MASTERING CRYPTO 2021

This book includes:

BLOCKCHAIN TECHNOLOGY EXPLAINED

& BITCOIN AND CRYPTOCURRENCY TRADING. A Beginner's Guide About Definitions, Crypto Exchanges, Indicator and Trading Tips

Warren Larsen

BOOK 1: BLOCKCHAIN TECHNOLOGY EXPLAINED

BOOK 2: BITCOIN AND CRYPTOCURRENCY TRADING

TABLE OF CONTENTS

BLOCKCHAIN TECHNOLOGY EXPLAINED

2021

The Ultimate Beginner's Guide About Blockchain
Wallet, Mining, Bitcoin, Ethereum, Litecoin,
Monero, Ripple, Dash, IOTA and More

By

Warren Larsen

1

Blockchain Technology Explained 2021:

The Ultimate Beginner's Guide About Blockchain Wallet, Mining,

Bitcoin, Ethereum, Litecoin, Monero, Ripple, Dash, IOTA and More

Written by WARREN LARSEN.

Errors and Feedback

Contact us if you find any errors

INTRODUCTION

The birth of Bitcoin in 2009, and the subsequent development of other cryptocurrencies in the following years, were the most important events in the world of alternative finance. Cryptocurrencies are a complex phenomenon, of international and interdisciplinary importance, which touches on economic, mathematical, jurisprudential, political and social issues.

The interest in cryptocurrencies has manifested itself both with regards to "blockchain" technology, and for the possibility of making payments without the intermediation of third parties (banks and financial intermediaries in general). The evolution of this market, however, must be inextricably linked to a financial investment context.

The interest in this "world" was amplified by the global economic-financial situation, characterized by particularly low interest rates, and due to the expansionary monetary policies adopted by the Central Banks in response to the 2007 crisis. A situation like this has led investors to be more demanding in seeking alternative finance situations that are capable of satisfying their desire for return. For these reasons, many subjects have seen cryptocurrencies as a "financial product", understood with the more generic meaning of investment opportunities, adequate to meet their needs. After having looked at the historical and systemic context that allowed the birth of the first cryptocurrency, Bitcoin, the aim of this thesis is to analyze the investment possibilities in this market.

First of all, through a theoretical study of the functioning of cryptocurrencies, and secondlyin a practical way, through a real investment with the creation of a portfolio.

The first chapter of the thesis deals with the phenomenon of cryptocurrencies, in general at first and then focusing in particular on the Bitcoin technology. Bitcoin, as the first cryptocurrency, deserves special consideration and a more accurate and complete analysis that will be reserved for subsequent cryptocurrencies.

For this reason, all of the issues in the first chapter

concerning its functioning, will be touched upon; from the main purpose intended by the creator of Bitcoin Satoshi Nakamoto, to the revolutionary technology of the blockchain. Particular attention will also be paid to those who work for the operation of the Bitcoin network, the so-called "Miners", and for those who allow the exchange of cryptocurrencies into fiat currencies and vice versa, the so-called "exchanges", right up to where Bitcoin is held in the various types of wallets (wallets).

The second chapter deals with introducing and classifying cryptocurrencies that were developed after Bitcoin. The classification is carried out both by taking into account the objective pursued by the developers and creators of the "coins", and by studying the peculiarities of the technology underlying the cryptocurrencies. An analysis of the market trend as well as a comparison with Bitcoin, will also be presented for each cryptocurrency, in order to identify the differences. The choice of Bitcoin as a reference and comparison "coin" is undoubtedly linked to the fact that it is still the most important and well-known cryptocurrency. As well as the one that dominates (in technical terms precisely the "dominance") the sector from the point of view of the capitalization market.

CHAPTER 1
CRYPTOCURRENCIES AND BITCOIN

In recent years, a payment system has emerged that is closely linked to information technology and the web network. The Internet was the most important innovation that involved the 20th century in a way that influenced all aspects of reality. A general change in social, economic, political and legal has taken place on the large scale of everyday life, with a gradual and disruptive infiltration.

In this constantly evolving context, banks have also had to adapt to changes, updating and sometimes revolutionizing their payment systems, in order to make them more effective and efficient in allowing quick and secure online transactions.

The world of payment systems and finance is transforming before our eyes. Digitized resources and channels, new financial instruments and systems are creating new methodologies for financial transactions and capital investments. Cryptocurrencies, also known as virtual currencies, are part of this process of innovation and technological adaptation.

WHAT ARE CRYPTOCURRENCIES?

Bitcoin has been in use since January 2009, and was the first cryptocurrency. The second cryptocurrency, Namecoin, emerged only two years later, in April 2011. Since then, thousands of virtual currencies have emerged, and hundreds of them can be traded on exchanges and have a considerable value and market capitalization.

The answer to the question of what cryptocurrencies are is neither simple nor trivial. A cryptocurrency is a cryptographic asset (asset, in the broadest meaning of the term), in the sense that it uses cryptography to guarantee the security of its transactions, of a digital type, which is used as an exchange asset between subjects operating in the network. It is said that cryptocurrencies are generic "assets" because from the current regulation and their usage, it is not yet possible to specifically establish which category of assets they fall into. On the one hand, cryptocurrencies may seem like assets similar to "coins", as they are used for the purchase of other assets. On the other hand, as will be analyzed later in the thesis, they have characteristics and uses similar to those of financial assets, in the sense that they are put into circulation by companies, as means for financing the companies themselves; a function similar to the share market, without allowing those who buy them to become owners (shareholders) of the company in question.

The common element of these different virtual currencies is precisely the blockchain technology, a public "ledger" that allows users to participate in the network and manage it in the absence of a central authority. The wide potential of application of the blockchain, in various disciplinary areas, is perhaps the aspect that has aroused the most interest in the events that have brought cryptocurrencies to the fore.

Virtual currencies are digital, equal and decentralized. Decentralization lies in the fact that, unlike all traditional currencies, cryptocurrencies do not have a central body that deals with their issue,there is no Central Bank that controls its value and no intermediaries that are required for the validation of transactions. Cryptocurrencies use cryptographic principles for the validation of operations, and for the creation of the money itself; carried out through a process of small but continuous "monetary expansion" over time. The joint process of "creation" of the cryptocurrency and validation of operations, is carried out thanks to the work of the "miners", their task will be further analyzed in a later chapter.

Given the historical location of their advent, it can be said that cryptocurrencies are a response both to the financial and economic crisis that began in 2007, and the need for a unit of account is linked directly to the interconnected world.

The main innovation of cryptocurrencies concerns being able to use the principles of cryptography with a digital currency whose amount is limited. Although bitcoin only started operating at the beginning of 2009, the concept of cryptocurrency has more distant origins, and has developed over time in a progressive manner, taking advantage of new technologies and needs born following the development of the Internet.

First of all, it is appropriate to identify the common aspects that bind all virtual currencies and retrace the history that led to the birth in 2008 , and the use of it starting from 2009 of the first cryptocurrency: bitcoin.

CRYPTOCURRENCIES IN BRIEF

A first linguistic misunderstanding that needs to be clarified, is the difference between the concept of electronic money (through which an electronic payment is made), and that of cryptocurrency (digital money). The two terms may seem synonymous but in reality they are not at all. When we talk about electronic money or currency,we are referring to what in English is called ecash. The term concerns the currency that is used on the web to make payments, which takes place through legal tender currencies.

Purchases that take place on the web require an electronic payment, a payment without the physical transfer of money. The operation of these transactions is essentially similar for all companies that deal with these type of payments. Firstly, a deposit account is opened and an amount of physical money is paid in with an intermediary. Through the account you can make payments via the Internet in all stores on the web. Each time a payment is made, the amount spent online is deducted from the deposit, and the company transfers it to the recipient's account. Using electronic money is essentially equivalent to making payments through the use of dematerialized fiat money, without the need for an actual passage between those who carry out the transaction.

Cryptocurrencies are the first form of "digital cash", they combine the advantages of electronic money and cash. Like a bank transfer, they allow remote payments; but at the same time, similar to a payment made in cash, they guarantee the instantaneousness of the operation and involve no costs for either, the person making the payment or the person receiving it.

Cryptocurrencies, like a banknote, are anonymous; that is, they do not require the identities of those carrying out the transaction, or the cause of the payment to be disclosed. But, being digital and divisible almost indefinitely, they allow transfers for any amount, from the payment of a few cents, to the regulation of international commercial traffic. Like a payment card, they allow you to pay any amount in real time and securely anywhere in the world. However, in analogy with cash, they allow the subjects carrying out the transaction to remain anonymous.

THE CONCEPT OF CRYPTOCURRENCY

The first person to talk about cryptocurrencies was David Lee Chaum in 1982, when he published an article entitled "Blind Signatures for Untraceable Payments", here he introduced the concept of virtual currency. The publication was not successful at first, probably because the times were not yet ready, and for a long time it was neglected and associated mostly with the chyperpunk movement.

In 1990 Chaum founded the company Digicash in Amsterdam in the Netherlands, who were chosen for their advantageous legislative structure for this type of activity. Digicash aspired to integrate cryptography with money, pursuing the aim of making transactions anonymous. In 1994, thanks to Digicash, the first electronic payment was made. Despite the positive start, the company closed in 1999 due to economic problems. Although he was the first to introduce the concept of cryptocurrency, Chaum with his company did not develop one, but dealt with electronic money.

SATOSHI NAKAMOTO, THE BITCOIN

Satoshi Nakamoto's article, referred to in the previous paragraph, talks about a decentralized and purely peer-to-peer virtual currency (PTP or P2P) that allows online payments without going through an intermediary.

The expression PTP indicates a logical architecture model of a computer network, whose nodes are arranged in hierarchical order through equal forms. which Designed to act as both server and customer (client or fixed server) to the other end nodes of the network. The key thing that sets this network apart is that every node is able to initiate or complete a transaction.

Decentralization lies in the fact that in bitcoin, unlike other traditional currencies, there is no central body that controls and manages the issue, regulating the functioning and work of those who perform the function of intermediaries.

The European Central Bank (ECB) is the central body that controls the euro through a monetary policy in the countries of the Euro Zone; similarly, the Federal

Reserve (Fed) control the US dollar. For bitcoin, on the other hand, there is no subject, be it a public body or a private body, to perform this function. Despite this, saying that the Bitcoin network has no control is profoundly wrong, in fact control exists. It is widespread (in the sense that it is shared among the network participants), and distributed in the network, guaranteed by adherence to a common protocol.

The protocol is formed by a set of rules that define the functioning of the system, and that apply in the functioning of the Bitcoin software. All hardware devices in which the Bitcoin software operates (technically defined as "network nodes"), can communicate through the network with other devices, thus actively managing the cryptocurrency. The greater the number of nodes joining the network, the more the "decentralization" becomes significant and effective.

Since the software and protocol were conceived and released by the inventor of Bitcoin (Satoshi Nakamoto), some skeptics think that the "control" and central authority of the currency is in the hands of the creator himself. This however is disproved by the nature of the

Bitcoin project being an open-source as well as the software being "open" to developers who want to make improvements. However, it is impossible for the developers themselves to force a drastic change to the software, as each node can freely choose which version of the software to use, provided that it is compliant and compatible with the software used by the other nodes. Basically, the consent between users and developers of the system is necessary for it to function properly.

To overcome the lack of centralized control, a peer-to-peer network is used and a digital signature is required to complete any cryptocurrency transactions. The P2P network is used to carry out "time stamps" to affix the application of an alphanumeric algorithm. As a reward to the node that first manages to execute the algorithm, a quantity of bitcoin is released, this process in IT terms is called "hash", and essentially consists in the transformation through an injective (noninvertible) function of a sequence of characters of arbitrary length (commonly know as a message) in a predefined length sequence called "hash value" or "message digest".

MAIN CHARACTERISTICS OF THE

17

BITCOIN

Under the European Central Bank directive "Virtual Currency Schemes - A further Analysis" of 2015, bitcoin is defined as an unregulated digital currency used among members of a virtual community. Bitcoin is a virtual currency that is exchanged at any time, with both incoming and outgoing fiat coins (it can be purchased with fiat coins and transformed into fiat coins).

The main features are:

DECENTRALIZATION:

Bitcoin was neither established nor controlled by any central authority. The transaction control is carried out by many independent subjects (the nodes). In this way the presence of intermediaries is not necessary for the carrying out of cryptocurrency transfers.

INDEPENDENCE AND NON-SUBJECTION TO MONETARY POLICY:

The absence of a central authority means that the circulation of money cannot be increased or decreased at will, such as what occurs in the monetary policy of

18

central banks. The money supply is established a priori by the protocol, it increases in a manner before

decreasing until the maximum threshold of pre-established units of 21 million bitcoins is reached.

The increase in working capital occurs every time an algorithm is executed, in this case through the so-called mining, which makes it possible to operate the system. Each time an algorithm is executed, a reward for this is given to the "miner", that receives in exchange, an amount X of newly issued bitcoins predetermined by the protocol.The quantity X is the commissions of those who carry out transactions in that period. For example, a subject A who transfers 1 bitcoin (BTC in abbreviation) to a subject B, can decide to leave a commission of 0.0001 BTC to the miners. The sum of all the commissions left, is attributed to the miner who first executes the algorithm.

For the first four years after the creation of bitcoin, the amount X decided as a reward for the resolution of the algorithm, was 50 bitcoins. Every 4 years the amount of bitcoin issued after each operation is reduced by 50%. So from 2013 until 2017, the premium for mining was 25 BTC. At this time and for the next 2 years, 12.5 bitcoins will be issued for each execution of the algorithm. The execution of the algorithm occurs every about 10 minutes; this time period is established by the system, and is kept the same because every two weeks, the algorithm is calibrated to ensure that this period of time is respected. As a consequence of this choice, the increase in working capital grows, following a geometric series that tends asymptotically to 21 million.

ANONYMITY:

Transactions take place between "public addresses" from which it is impossible to trace the real natural person who operates through that pseudonym. Public addresses are essentially points of receipt and sending of BTC, which can be assimilated to a sort of banking IBAN.

TRANSPARENCY:

All transactions are recorded in public records that areaccessible to anyone, known as the blockchains. By exploring the blockchains, it is possible to know how many bitcoins a public address may have and also which
20

other address has provided them. Simply put, it is as if every time a bitcoin transaction occurs, that transaction remains forever recorded in the bitcoin itself. Despite this transparency, that will be explained later, it is not possible to reach the natural person from the public key.

LOW TRANSACTION COSTS:

The cost for each operation carried out in bitcoins is free, as each user can decide the amount when carrying out the operation. Despite this freedom, commissions are usually around 0.00001BTC. Making the so-called "donations" to the miners of lower amounts, risky for the actual success of the transaction, especially if there are many operations within the 10 minutes in which you make your own. As miners are responsible for authenticating transactions, they can choose which transactions to include in their block. One block, as will be explained later on, represents a "container" within which all of the bitcoin operations carried out in the considered time frame are entered. Each block can contain a number of limited transactions, where the maximum value is 4200; for this reason transactions with low commissions, can be left until last, if in the period in which they are made there are more than 4200 transactions made through BTC.

Much higher costs are those commissions that are placed by the exchanges that deal with the transformation of the Dollar, Euro and other legal tender currencies into bitcoin and vice versa. Although it should be noted that exchanges take enormous risks when dealing with cryptocurrencies, given the very high volatility that characterizes this market, as well as the lack of clear legislation.

SECURITY AND SPEED OF TRANSACTIONS:

Each bitcoin transaction takes an average of 10 minutes to be made, these transactions are irreversible and are impossible to cancel.

THE BLOCKCHAIN

The Blockchain is the computer equivalent of a public ledger in all Bitcoin transactions that have been performed up to now. It can be thought of as a "chain" formed by a set of "blocks", which in turn are formed by a set of transactions. The "chain" has the characteristic of recording and filing all transactions carried out within the network, without the need for a third party to manage the system. The "ledger" is constantly growing, recording any data relating to all operations.

The data is equipped with a defense mechanism, based on encryption, against tampering or the possibility of modification. Transactions take place continuously in the network, while the blocks are "hooked" to the chain, on an average of every ten minutes. Each block is arranged on the chain in a chronological sequence starting from the original block , the so-called "genesis block".

A block is the current part of the blockchain, it can be seen as a "container" inside of which all transactions awaiting authentication are stored. The number of data that can be entered in each single block is defined and limited, as already mentioned, to a maximum of 4200 transactions; one every seven seconds or so. Each block is filled with accounting records, coinciding with the individual transactions (for example A transfers the number of bitcoins to B), which operate in a similar way to a banking IBAN. Once completed and authenticated, the block is linked to the blockchain and remains permanently recorded in the database (the transaction cannot be canceled in any way). The global network of nodes carries out the chaining every 10 minutes, before the authentication of the new block, it verifies the effective connection of all of the blocks of the chain (all of the blocks from the genesis block up to the last authenticated block).

Through the mechanism just described above, it is possible to verify at any time, that the transactions have taken place correctly, so that each bitcoin is transferred only once, avoiding the so-called "double spending". In this way, the functioning of the blockchain prevents a subject from sending the same bitcoin to two different individuals. Each node (i.e. all computers connected to the Bitcoin network), holds a copy of the blockchain, which is automatically downloaded by each miner who joins the Bitcoin network.

The Blockchain is a system where the smallest particle is the single transaction, the basic accounting entry where the set of several transactions form a block and the set of all the blocks form the chain.

Until a few years ago, the blockchain was used only

for the operation of the Bitcoin network, in the sense that all the possible application areas, to which such a technology could have been applied, had not yet been identified. In recent years, however, interest in this technology has increased and there could be many future applications. From this perspective, the birth of many cryptocurrencies should be read, interesting not so much for the currencies themselves, but rather for the technologies that underlie the actual cryptocurrencies. In fact, very often companies that are involved in developing a blockchain "create" their own currency (this will be analyzed in the second chapter).

Blockchain has the same importance and function that IPO30 (Initial Public Offering) have for normal companies; to raise capital to reinvest for the development of the company itself. For this reason, blockchain technology has been met with great interest from financial giants and very often from institutions. This suggests that in the future, the "chain" can be applied in finance (the so-called FINTECH).

Therefore, in the near future, the use of the blockchain could be fundamental for the transmission of information between financial intermediaries, and the various supervisory authorities. On the one hand, leading to facilitating control and compliance procedures and, on the other, to greater efficiency and speed of supervision.

In addition to financial applications, the applications of the blockchain can be many others and move on an interdisciplinary field. Great importance could have an application in contracts in the phenomenon known as REGTECH, contraction of Regulation and Technology, that is the use of technological tools to support the procedures of adjustment, compliance, regulations, laws, reporting.

To better understand how the blockchain works, it is necessary to introduce the concept of "mining" and the function performed by the so-called "miners".

THE BLOCKCHAIN AND CRYPTOGRAPHY

The security of the blockchain comes from the type of cryptography it uses. Each transaction recorded on the blockchain is encrypted and only its recipient is able to decrypt it. In this way, the blockchain does not need to implement particular security systems to "defend" a

26

data, as this is made indecipherable by all those who are not authorized to do so. This was made possible by employing asymmetric cryptography.

HOW DOES ASYMMETRIC ENCRYPTION WORK?

Asymmetric cryptography is based on the use of a pair of keys: a public key and a private key. The key pair is mathematically linked by a function, this ensures that a message encrypted with one of the two keys can only be decrypted by the other.

Let's take an example to clarify what has just been said. We have two people: A and B. A wants to send a text document to B, but wants to make sure that only B can read the contents of that document. A then decides to use asymmetric cryptography, therefore uses B's public key to encrypt his message (A knows B's public key because, being public, B has made it available to A). The document thus encrypted can no longer be decrypted by A, as it is not in possession of B's private key (this, unlike the public key, is indeed private: only B has it). B receives the document and manages to decrypt it using his private key. Once B has received and

27

opened the document, he decides to reply to A using the same encryption method, so as to be sure that only he can read the contents of his document. It then encrypts the document using A's public key. A receives the document and manages to decrypt it using his private key.

How asymmetric encryption works is as simple as it is effective. You should have understood that anyone with the public key used to encrypt a message, will not be able to decrypt it, the only way to do this is to use the private key associated with the public key used. This mechanism is not effective if used in reverse, as if you were to encrypt a message using the private key, anyone with the associated public key would be able to decrypt it.

THE MINING AND THE MINERS

"Miners" play a crucial role in any cryptocurrency system. They are the subjects that allow the operation of the Bitcoin network and, through their active participation, guarantee the security of the protocol. Miners are responsible for grouping and authenticating transactions that take place via bitcoin. Their activity consists in solving the "hashes" for the authentication of transactions and operations, therefore they have a function of "notaries", in the sense that they certify the validity of the bitcoin transfer procedures, by creating new blocks to add to the " ledger "(the blockchain).

The miners also provide the computing power necessary to protect the blockchain from possible attempts to subvert and centralize its operation. New blocks are added at constant times. To guarantee the timing, the protocol provides that the difficulty of solving the hashes depends on the number of subjects that are involved in the mining. Regardless of how many transactions take place in the system, every two weeks, according to the Bitcoin protocol, on average 2016 new blocks must be produced, about 1 every 10 minutes, even if no one carries out any transactions. Every two weeks, if the new blocks produced deviate from the target number of 2016, the production difficulty of a new block is revised up or down, depending on whether the output of new blocks was lower or higher to 2016. The difficulty of producing the block depends on the ease with which the hash function can be performed.

If the number of subjects increases, the difficulty of solving the hash increases accordingly, because by increasing the computer power, the miners involved in solving a hash will take less time to find the solution. Since the Bitcoin operation requires that the solutions are "found" every 10 minutes, it is necessary that the hash is adequate for the number of participants in the operations of applying the hash function. The correct solution for the continuation of the blockchain is selected by the protocol, and as a reward for its generation, the miner who solved it receives X amount of new generation bitcoins, plus the sum of all the commissions that have been affixed in block operations.

The commissions, while free, must have an adequate amount. In fact, miners can decide which transactions to enter in the authentication, given that the protocol has a maximum number of authentications with a single validation operation (about 4200 transactions). Presumably miners will choose to authenticate trades with more generous fees first. This way a fee of less than 0.00001 BTC risks taking a longer time to authenticate. The payment of a "prize" reserved for the miners who support the network, was designed to discourage attempts at centralizing the system, which would only be possible with the consent of the majority of the platform participants. Since there is a reward for their work, it is convenient for the miners not to subvert the system and continue to work for its maintenance.

In the beginning, mining could be done with a normal computer. However, as the number of participants in the network increases, this function can only be performed with expensive and sophisticated machinery, designed and created specifically to perform this function. Nowadays, in reality, not even these types of devices guarantee efficiency in resolving hashes. The energy cost to power this type of tool is considerable, for this reason very often the minators come together to increase the probability of being able to solve the hashes and continue the blockchain. The so-called "mining pool" was born from the everincreasing difficulty of being able to "mine" efficiently.

In fact, mining of the most important crypto is now almost an exclusive of mining "giants". These are groups of miners organized with the aim of dividing the computational capacity to be able to execute the various hashes of cryptocurrencies with higher probability.

WALLETS

Bitcoin wallets are similar to a checking account. They provide information at all times regarding the "content" of the wallet and the entry and exit operations in the wallet, as a sort of account statement in real time. Despite this similarity with current accounts, bitcoins are not really contained within the wallet, but are stored in a public register (the blockchain) under specific addresses belonging to different users. The addresses are receiving and sending points consisting essentially of alphanumeric codes of 33 or 34 characters, the first of which is always a "1".

Each code does not contain any information regarding the customer, and being one random combination of numbers and letters, it cannot in any way refer to the user. This feature makes Bitcoin a completely anonymous payment method, through which users make payments with pseudonyms.

Bitcoin transactions are based on the mechanism of

"asymmetric transactions", also called public key mechanism - private key. The two keys are alphanumeric codes through which it is possible to perform operations on the Bitcoin platform. Each user holds a pair of keys, one public and one private. The addresses mentioned earlier, derive algorithmically from public keys, which in turn derive through a non-injective function from private keys. Basically, with this mechanism you can get from the private key to the public one, but not vice versa. From the public key, it is impossible to reach the private one; in this sense the transaction mechanism is defined asymmetric. Through the mechanism just described, starting from the address it is impossible to reach the original keys (both the public key or the private key) and consequently the user of the wallet.

The user is authorized to use the bitcoins present in their wallet only at the moment in which it is in possession of its private reference key. It is therefore necessary that the private key must be kept with the utmost confidentiality and not be lost. Each time a new wallet is generated, one hundred (100) public keys are created, that refer to a single private key (kay-pool). This way, the user can take advantage of 100 different addresses connected to the same wallet. Privacy is guaranteed through this mechanism because, even if someone were able to associate a subject with a public key (which is very difficult), it would be impossible for them to trace the other operations carried out by the same subject, as any other movement could be carried out with another 99 keys.

Although this type of operation may seem complex, in reality they are carried out entirely by the system. The wallet is, in fact, quite simple and intuitive and does not differ much from a reserved area of a bank website.

It is possible to have different types of wallets which depend on the level of practicality and safety that the user wants to have. The first wallet, the most common one, is the "desktop wallet". It consists of software being installed on your computer. This type of wallet can be risky, if you do not pay due attention by entering periodically changed passwords, and having an updated antivirus system, your computer could be hacked. In this way it would be possible to recover the private key and therefore steal the bitcoins held in the wallet.

The "mobile wallet" is similar to the "desktop wallet", the only difference is that it is installed as an application on your smartphone. The same goes for the "tablet wallet" which, as is evident from the name, will be installed on your tablet.

Some argue that this is the riskiest way, but perhaps more practical and faster. Other's advise to keep your bitcoins through the online wallet. This type of service is usually provided by exchanges, the online trading platforms that deal with exchanging bitcoin and other cryptocurrencies with fiat currency. As there have been some cases of attacks on exchange platform servers, holding bitcoin online is strongly discouraged.

The last category of wallet is the hardware one; it consists of a device created specifically to keep the private keys of bitcoin addresses and other crypto. This type of wallet connects to the computer via USB (usually a USB stick or hard drive), and thus interact with the wallet software in total safety. Once the operation has been carried out, the hardware wallet can be extracted from the computer device. In this way it will not be possible for any hacker to enter the wallet, being a wallet disconnected from the network. This method of "conservation" of the bitcoin wallet, although less practical to use, is undoubtedly the safest, and gives the user the certainty that their bitcoins are not stolen.

A research study, conducted by the University of Cambridge for the "Alternative Finance" department in September in 2020 by Garrick Hilleman & Michel Rauchs, found that the use of wallets on phones, is the most frequent with 65% of users holding their own cryptocurrencies in this type of wallet, in comparison to only 23% who use hardware wallets (the safest method for holding cryptocurrencies).

MOBILE WALLET	65%
DESKTOP WALLET	42%
WEB WALLET	38%
TABLET WALLET	31%
HARDWARE WALLET	23%

While it may seem like a trivial statistic, it is not at all. Such a distributed use of portfolios may lead us to think, as the Cambridge researchers also underlined, that the interest in cryptocurrencies is to be framed in speculative and financial investment operations. In fact, holding cryptocurrencies in a "mobile wallet", allows users to be able to sell and buy them more quickly than other systems, which are considered safer. As will be analyzed later in the manuscript, the use of cryptocurrencies has taken a different turn than the one that the creator of Bitcoin had originally thought. In fact, they are considered by users to be "financial products", in the broadest sense of the term, ie they are perceived as an investment opportunity.

THE EXCHANGES

To operate through cryptocurrencies, it is almost always necessary to go through bitcoins, which are recognized by all as the most important and most liquid crypto, recommended as the easiest way to transform into fiat money. The purchase of bitcoins can take place in two ways; either through a direct exchange between a subject who holds bitcoins, wants to sell them and who wants to buy them, or through the intermediation of an exchange.

Direct exchange can also be organized through sites

which can consequently be considered exchanges, dealing with putting in contact those who are interested in selling or buying bitcoins. The exchange can take place both online, through payments with bank transfers, or through meetings and electronic payments in physical presence.

The meetings obviously take place in places with internet connection and are often organized by the same site. As for the localbitcoins.com site, it is active in 15962 cities and 248 countries, including Italy, making it the leading site in the sector.

The sites that deal with exchanges in physical presence between subjects in Italy, have numerous locations; especially in the north, where they are present in almost all of the former provincial capitals. The cities with multiple locations are: Milan, Turin and Rome.

In any case, the most common way to buy and sell your bitcoins remains to rely on an online intermediary, the real exchange. The exchanges provide services for the trading of cryptocurrencies with legal tender currencies. The role of exchange is fundamental for the virtual currency market, because they guarantee a market for trading and its liquidity and consequently the possibility of creating a price for the various crypto. They essentially have a function of a Market Maker, that is that of an intermediary who "decides" what the prices should be of a purchase and sale of a specific asset.

Exchanges were the first phenomenon that developed following the birth of bitcoin. The first, "Bitcoin Market", was opened on February 6, 2010, since then hundreds of them have been born and the exchange sector is the most important in terms of volumes and activity.

Exchanges can be divided into two groups; those that operate mainly through bitcoins and those that allow a quick transition from various cryptocurrencies to fiat currencies. The former allow the exchange of bitcoins in all other cryptocurrencies, and the person who intends to operate there must therefore own bitcoins and pay them into the exchange account. Once the bitcoins have been deposited in the exchange account, they will be able to purchase all of the cryptocurrencies supported by the platform through bitcoins.

Taking an example; if Luigi wants to buy X units of

Litecoin in an exchange that operates only through Bitcoins, he will have to hold enough bitcoins in his exchange account to buy the desired Litecoin. The exchange therefore takes place between Bitcoin and Litecoin. If Luigi wanted to buy another crypto with his Litecoins, he would have to change those Litecoins into Bitcoins and then with Bitcoins buy the desired cryptocurrency. Even if Luigi wants to exchange his Litecoin for fiat currency (dollar or euro), he should first switch to Bitcoins.

When making a cryptocurrency exchange, commissions will obviously be provided for. The use of Bitcoin as a cryptocurrency is due to the fact that Bitcoin is the best known cryptocurrency, with a higher market capitalization and higher liquidity. In other exchanges, it is instead possible to go directly from fiat currency (dollar more commonly or in some cases even euro) to cryptocurrency and vice versa.

KIND OF ACTIVITY'	DESCRIPTION
Order-Book Exchange	Platform that matches users' purchase and sales orders. It can also facilitate the physical

	meeting of subjects and the direct exchange of cryptocurrencies.
Brokerage Service	Service that allows users to acquire and / or sell cryptocurrencies at a given price.
Trading Platform	Platform that allows you to buy cryptocurrencies or ETFs of the same, even in leverage. The user works only with the platform, there are no operations between users.

The Order-Book Exchange does not buy cryptocurrencies on its own, but combines buy and sell orders, their income derives solely from commissions. In essence, the exchange does not expose itself in the first person in the purchase and sale of cryptocurrencies, the transaction is carried out by the two subjects directly. The intermediary only makes them "meet". This type of function can also be aimed at the physical meeting of people who want to exchange cryptocurrencies, in the way that has been explained above.

The "Brokerage Service" is the real "Broker" function. The intermediary receives a buy and sell order from the user and "goes to the market" to execute it. Also in this case, the risk is minimal and the gain comes from commissions.

The last type of exchange is the more risky one, the "Trading Platform" hold cryptocurrencies in their wallets and make the purchase or sale as a direct seller or buyer of the customer. The platform is one of the two parties carrying out the operation (either the seller or the buyer). In this last case of exchange, the platform assumes a very high risk, because it exposes itself to the possibility that cryptocurrencies depreciate or revalue; the risk is furthermore accentuated by the very high volatility that characterizes the cryptocurrency market. From this perspective, the considerable commissions required in each operation should be read.Here they are around 3.5% for each operation, both for purchase and sale. In addition to a higher purchase or sale price, in the case of purchase, or lower.

After having identified and briefly analyzed the world of cryptocurrencies, dwelling on the pivotal moments of their birth and on the characteristics of the first cryptocurrency, Bitcoin, the goal of the next chapter will be to select and explain the distinctive features of the main cryptocurrencies that are traded in the market right now. It is necessary to focus on them to analyze the technological innovations they have developed with respect to Bitcoin, and in particular the innovations regarding the blockchain. As explained later, other blockchain technologies have arisen which, although starting from the same assumptions, differ substantially from the technology that is the basis of Bitcoin, and have had considerable interest in the potential areas of application to which they can be adapted.

CHAPTER 2
THE MAIN CRYPTOCURRENCIES

The main feature of the Bitcoin project is that it is open-source, to allow anyone participating in the network to introduce improvements to the platform. While on the one hand, this feature was one of its strengths, through which it was possible to continuously improve and make the network more efficient with the contribution of developers from all over the world, on the other hand, it proved to be a weakness because it has made it possible to create new cryptocurrencies competing with BTC; which, in a different way, exploited the public information underlying the Bitcoin platform.

The cryptocurrencies created after Bitcoin, can be divided into three groups: the "Altcoins" (or "Alternative Coins", alternatives to Bitcoin), the "Innovative Cryptocurrencies" and the "Cryptocurrency platforms". The former are developed either directly by Bitcoin with a "fork" of the project, that is an "expansion" of a new software project that starts from the source code of an existing one (in this case from that of Bitcoin), or they are developed from the beginning, retracing or even copying, almost entirely the BTC protocol.

The Altcoins therefore can be described as cryptocurrencies that do not introduce substantial or important innovations, to either the Bitcoin procedure or the blockchain; they are basically copies of Bitcoin. Hundreds of examples of altcoins can be found. To name a few, we can mention: "Namecoin" the second cryptocurrency, born from a fork of Bitcoin in April 2011, "Dogecoin", "Dash" or the more recent "Bitcoin Cash". As already mentioned, Altcoins do not present substantial improvements to Bitcoin, but some of them have the objective of overcoming some shortcomings of Bitcoin technology, from the point of view of efficiency. Just to give an example, the times required for a Bitcoin transfer are relatively long if we consider those used by cryptocurrencies born later.

The "Innovative Cryptocurrencies", unlike the Altcoin, are virtual currencies whose operation, although starting from the principles of Bitcoin, is innovative. The innovation may lie in the fact that the blockchain is conceived in a different way, as in the case of "Iota", or other characteristics of the cryptocurrency may differ substantially. This is the case of "Ripple" which, for example, is a centralized cryptocurrency, in the sense that it is controlled by a central third party.

Finally, the "Cryptocurrency platforms", such as "Ethereum", explained later, allow the creation of "smart contracts". Ethereum is the second largest cryptocurrency by market capitalization after Bitcoin, and is considered, due to the substantial innovation it has introduced, as a 2.0 cryptocurrency. The substantial innovation of Ethereum lies in the fact that, in addition to being a cryptocurrency, it is also a platform within which "applications" can be developed and can run other cryptocurrencies.

All cryptocurrencies are a platform (even Bitcoin is), but such a platform can be used exclusively for transactions that take place through the cryptocurrency that was born on that specific platform. The "Cryptocurrencies 2.0", on the other hand, have a platform programmed to be shared with those who want to use it It is therefore used for both, the transactions of the main cryptocurrency of the platform, and as a platform suitable for exercising the functions described above. The functioning of the Ethereum platform and of the cryptocurrency 2.0 platforms in general will be explained later in this chapter.

In addition to the distinction made above, a further differentiation of crypto must be introduced, based no longer on the underlying technology, but on the platform on which they operate. From this point of view, there are two types of cryptocurrencies: "Coins" and "Tokens". The "Coins" are independent cryptocurrencies, whose functioning does not depend on any other cryptocurrency, they have their own blockchain and their own network. The "Tokens", on the contrary, are cryptocurrencies that operate on the same platform as a "Coin", and substantially depend directly on that "Coin". Tokens do not have their own blockchain or platform, but are developed within the blockchain and the platform of a Coin. This type of cryptocurrency can only be developed within a cryptocurrency 2.0 platform, i.e. crypto such as Ethereum or NEO.

Just to give an example, consider the NEO cryptocurrency, which will be covered later. Those who own NEO, are assigned a proportional amount of another crypto, NEO's "Token", the "GAS" to predefine periods of time. Therefore, with mechanisms like this, a sort of "dividend" in the form of another cryptocurrency "Token" than the one held, is attributed to the owner of a specific crypto. Other Tokens, running within the platform of a Coin, can be developed independently from the Coin; without being generated and provided as a "dividend" to the holders of the main Coin of the platform. An example of this can be EOS, the most important Token in terms of market capitalization, which was developed in the Ethereum platform, but independently of the Coin Ethereum. The platform that has the most success for its Token operation is undoubtedly Ethereum. If you visit the sitehttps://coinmarketcap.com/tokens/, eight of the first ten tokens based on the market capitalization "run" on the platform Ethereum.

Summarizing what has been said so far, cryptocurrencies differ in terms of innovative scope compared to Bitcoin in; "Altcoin", "Innovative cryptocurrencies" and "Platform cryptocurrencies". In turn, the "innovative cryptocurrencies" can be innovative in two respects: 1) in regards to the functioning of the blockchain, for example Iota and 2) in regards to the fundamental characteristic of decentralization, such as the case of Ripple which is a centralized crypto.

The last category is that of "Cryptocurrencies 2.0", for example Ethereum and NEO; as mentioned, they are not only cryptocurrencies but are also platforms within which it is possible to operate and develop "smart contracts", applications and other cryptocurrencies (the so-called Tokens). Cryptocurrencies operating within platforms of another cryptocurrency differ from regular cryptocurrencies. Traditional cryptocurrencies are defined as "Coin", ie those that have their own blockchain and their own platform within which they can operate independently. Whilst other, cryptocurrencies that work through a platform of others such as cryptocurrencies 2.0, are defined as "tokens", and therefore appear to be dependent on this platform.

Considering the turmoil that rages in the crypto world, I believe it is necessary to analyze the categories of cryptocurrencies one at a time, explaining their characteristics. For each crypto category analyzed, the main cryptocurrencies belonging to this category will also be studied.

CHARACTERISTICS OF CRYPTOCURRENCIES

Before proceeding with the explanation of the categories of cryptocurrencies, it is useful to introduce some fundamental concepts that will be used to analyze the various cryptocurrencies. First of all, it must be said that from here on all the data used and the information regarding market prices, market capitalization, trading volume, etc ... will refer to what is reported by the sitecoinmarketcap.com/. The choice of the site, the most authoritative and complete among those dealing with the cryptocurrency market, was almost mandatory. In fact, this site is the only one that provides information for approximately all of the 1500 cryptocurrencies

50

existing at this time. Even the Bloomberg platform, despite having been consulted for some comparisons and researches, does not provide the information on the cryptocurrencies considered in this book, with the same punctuality and completeness.

MARKET CAPITALIZATION

The first concept that will be used for the analysis of cryptocurrencies, is that of "Market Cap".

The market capitalization of the cryptocurrency is calculated by multiplying the number of units of cryptocurrency, in circulation with the average market price of that crypto.

It is possible to draw a parallel in this sense, with the market capitalization of shares traded on regulated markets. The market capitalization of cryptocurrencies is calculated in a similar way; in this sense, there is a tendency to equate cryptocurrencies with financial instruments used as shares. As will be later discussed, in reality, cryptocurrencies are by no means shares of the companies that issue them. Those who hold a cryptocurrency, in fact do not become the owners of that company, but simply own an "asset" issued by the company itself. This asset, however, is different from all assets known by law. It is neither a share, nor a bond, nor a hybrid financial instrument.

VOLUME OF TRADE

The volumes represent the set of trading operations carried out on a cryptocurrency in a given unit of time. With reference to securities traded on the regulated market, and consequently also to cryptocurrencies, volumes can be interpreted as the expression of the interest that investors place in a particular security or market.

The volumes are also an indicator in regards to the dynamism of the market and also provide information on the relationship that exists between supply and demand. In addition to this, the analysis of the market volume is interesting for the study of cryptocurrencies, because it provides an approximate indication of the liquidity of the digital currency in question.

According to technical analysts, volume is a measure of the intensity or pressure that underlies a trend. The higher the volume, the more reliable and lasting the trend will be. Some financial market observers attribute to these "physical" behaviors, imagining that the trajectories followed by prices on the chart are governed by laws similar to those that regulate the movement of a body in real space. Hence the belief that volumes, or rather their increase, is of greater importance in the early stages of an uptrend rather than a bearish one. The analysis of the trend of volumes can therefore provide a series of important signals of confirmation or uncertainty of the trend.

CIRCULATING SUPPLY

The last characteristic that will be considered is the currency in circulation. It indicates the number of cryptocurrency that has been issued. The most important feature of most cryptocurrencies is that they have a limited number of units that can be issued. For this reason, it is certainly important to take into account the amount of currency already issued; the closer you are to the maximum number envisaged for the cryptocurrency, the more you may be led to think that the value of the cryptocurrency can increase (and the asset is limited).

In a similar way, the maximum value of cryptocurrency units that can be reached must also be analyzed; the lower this number is, the more it is likely that the value of the cryptocurrency can be high (obviously the price depends above all on the validity and reliability of the cryptocurrency project in question and the trust that the market places on this project).

If we consider cryptocurrencies that have a very high circulation, the price per single cryptocurrency will tend to be lower. On the contrary, when a cryptocurrency has a low number of circulation its price will tend to be high. The working capital must therefore be assessed with two precautions; the first is to evaluate it in absolute value. (If the currency is "High" or "low" compared to that of other competing cryptocurrencies). Secondly, it must be evaluated in proportion to the maximum circulating available.

These are the three fundamental characteristics from a numerical point of view that can be analyzed in a cryptocurrency. The analysis can be limited only to these three aspects, which in any case are the most significant, above all due to the difficulty in finding other reliable data and for an adequate period of time.

THE ALTCOIN

Since the aim of this thesis is to analyze the possibilities of investing in cryptocurrencies, it is, in my opinion, necessary to identify which are the main "Altcoins", listing their main characteristics, strengths and weaknesses as well as any possible future developments, that could change the price or make it join the most widespread use.

To initially select the most important cryptocurrencies in an approximate way and in order to analyze them, their market capitalization, trading volumes and their presence in the various exchanges, their deal with coins are taken into account. Referring to market capitalization, the most important "Altcoin" is BITCOIN CASH, a cryptocurrency that occupies the fourth place in terms of classification according to market capitalization. The other Altcoins are LITECOIN (in fifth place in the market capitalization ranking), MONERO (in tenth place) and DASH (in eleventh place). All the "Altcoin" cryptocurrencies mentioned here will be examined in the following paragraphs in order of market capitalization.

BITCOIN CASH

Bitcoin Cash, https://www.bitcoincash.org/, was born as a "fork" of Bitcoin on 1 August 2017 (in reality we speak of a "hard fork" given the importance of the fork in question). This cryptocurrency aims to continue the Bitcoin project and overcome some inefficiencies. The developers

decided to make a similar amount of Bitcoin Cash available to everyone who held "Bitcoin" at the time of the fork. The cryptocurrency therefore depends on Bitcoin at its birth. The blockchain of the Bitcoin Cash binds to the Bitcoin Blockchain from the start. In the sense that until August 1, 2017, the blockchain of the two cryptocurrencies is the same, but from August 1,

2017 it starts an independent blockchain and operates completely unrelated to Bitcoin.

Although it was born as a fork of Bitcoin, and has been on the market for a limited period of time (less than a year), Bitcoin Cash immediately managed to reach a considerable price and in fact, quickly placed itself among the first places in cryptocurrencies in regards to market capitalization. Like most cryptocurrencies, Bitcoin Cash (BTCC in acronym) is characterized by considerable market volatility.

Bitcoin Cash is the result of a very long dispute between the programmers and developers of the Bitcoin network, over the overcoming of the so-called "Bitcoin Scalability Problem". The problem refers to the limited amount of transactions that can be made within the Bitcoin network. As already seen in the first chapter, the problem of the limited quantity of transactions that can be processed by the network, is linked to the fact that the blocks in the Bitcoin blockchain have a limited size and frequency, in particular: The dimensional problem concerns that a limited number (4200) of transactions per block can be validated in the Bitcoin network.

The problem of frequency is instead linked to the fact that the Bitcoin system provides for a block to be validated about every 10 minutes. This function is not editable, since it was designed by the creator of Bitcoin to ensure that the units of Bitcoin issued were limited. With the times indicated above, the maximum number of transactions that can be validated every second is 7. This can become a problem when more transactions take place than those that can be validated, because it could cause some transactions to

take a long time to validate, with the theoretical possibility that a transaction may never be.

Bitcoin Cash was basically created to solve this problem, and so all those who were in possession of Bitcoin also became owners of the same amount of Bitcoin Cash.

As happens in all forks, there has been a split in the blockchain which has therefore led to complete independence (from the split date 1 August 2017) between Bitcoin and Bitcoin Cash. The substantial difference lies in the fact that in BTCC each block has a much larger size, which allows you to perform more transactions within it.

LITECOIN

The fifth Altcoin by market capitalization is Litecoin. The cryptocurrency has been distributed since October 7, 2011 and as stated by the main page of its website, is "a decentralized global currency based on Bitcoin technology". Also with regards to the inventors of Litecoin, the aim of the project was to improve the technology of Bitcoin by overcoming some gaps in the latter. Litecoin software was first

deployed in October 2011 on the software project hosting platform "GitHub", by former Google employee, Charles Lee. The main characteristics of Litecoin, which differentiate it from Bitcoin, are the shorter period of time required for the validation of a block, and the significant increase in the number of cryptocurrency units provided by the system.

As for the first Litecoin innovation, it is aimed at solving the problem of the number of transactions that can be validated in each block and the validation duration of a block. By reducing the block validation times, it is possible to obtain an efficiency of the two problems described above.

A different argument must be made for the amount of Litecoin circulating units envisaged by the system. When Bitcoin reached a considerable price level, in terms of fiat currencies, it became increasingly difficult to use it as a means of payment but this problem arose not so much due to the impossibility of dividing Bitcoin as a percentage (Bitcoin is transferable up to the minimum unit of 0.000001).

As observed from the Litecoin site itself, it is a "copy" of Bitcoin. In fact, the site publicly states that the functioning of the cryptocurrency is the same. Litecoin, whose acronym is LTC, is therefore a P2P (peer-to-peer) cryptocurrency that is based on an open source system. Litecoin is currently the second largest virtual currency by market capitalization.

Like all cryptocurrencies, Litecoin is not issued by any central authority, but "comes to life" thanks to mining procedures. Through this activity, the so-called miners solve complex mathematical problems in exchange for cryptocurrencies. This is another of the characteristics that Litecoin has in common with Bitcoin and other virtual currencies in circulation.

The incentive for miners is 50 Litecoin for each successfully verified block. The reward in terms of Litecoin, as in the case of BTC, it halves every 4 years. Every 2.5 minutes, the network generates a so-called block that is added to the others and with them composes the blockchain, the public register of all transactions in Litecoin. As in the case of Bitcoin, the maximum number of Litecoin has already been established by the system and is 84 million.

At the time of the Litecoin's birth, its creator Charles Lee made a comparison between Bitcoin and Litecoin, comparing Bitcoin to gold and Litecoin to silver. This desire for comparison is also evident from the choice of the logos of the two cryptocurrencies; the first in gold color, the second characterized by silver gray. The comparison with gold and silver was made above all, to justify the existence of both cryptocurrencies; the two precious metals have the same safe-haven function and their different price is characterized by their different rarity (Litecoin was also voluntarily made less rare than Bitcoin). Lee wanted to send an important message, namely that of the possibility of coexistence of two very similar cryptocurrencies.

MONERO

Litecoin was the first Altcoin that met with great success and a limelight on an international level, so much so, that starting from 2013 it has often been the protagonist of articles by important newspapers such as the "Wall Street Journal" and "New York Times", which identified it as a possible alternative to Bitcoin, if not actually in some cases as his successor. After the interest that has developed in the world of "Alternative Coins", many programmers started working on and developing other crypto projects.

The programmers of alternative cryptocurrencies have considered it essential, for the development to distinguish each of them with a conceptual or programmatic distinctive trait, which could guarantee a characteristic of exclusivity to the new crypto.

One of these projects, which ended in early 2014, led to the birth of "Monero", XMR in acronym. The cryptocurrency was created starting from April 18, 2014, the most important developers are the Spaniards, Riccardo Spagni and Fransisco Cabañas.

At first the cryptocurrency was called "BitMonero", only later the initial "Bit" was lost to make way for simply "Monero". In the introductory video of the cryptocurrency, the Monero programmers insist on the importance of "Financial Privacy" and on the crypto slogan "You are your own bank".

Monero is a decentralized, digital and secure cryptocurrency, based on cryptographic technology

63

operated by a network of users, whose transactions are confirmed and immutably registered on the crypto blockchain. The three main features of Monero are: security, privacy and non-traceability.

The privacy of cryptocurrency is guaranteed by the fact that the functioning of the blockchain, although similar to that of Bitcoin, is not completely public. The origin, amount and destination of all transactions carried out are obfuscated. Therefore, Monero makes all the characteristics of Bitcoin its own without compromising the privacy and anonymity of transactions. In any case, there is the possibility of cryptographic technology being operated by a network of users whose transactions are confirmed and immutably registered on the crypto blockchain.

Potentially becoming, "Selectively Trasparent", meaning that it may be possible to decide to make one, some or all of their transactions visible, and it can also be chosen which subjects can see those transactions.

DASH

The last "Altcoin" that will be considered in this

thesis is Dash. Like Bitcoin, Dash is an open-source peer-to-peer cryptocurrency. Its creator and current CEO is Ryan Taylor, former manager of the US company McKinsey & Company. The digital currency was put into circulation starting from 18 January 2014 with the name of XCoin (XCO). On the 28th of the same month, the name was changed to DarkCoin, only to be changed again in March 2015 to Dash (from the English Digital Cash).

Despite having a similar operation to Bitcoin, Dash has introduced a series of improvements in the operation and speed of transactions.

From an "administrative" point of view, the functions

of Dash are different from those of Bitcoin.

There are two functions in the Dash networks; that of "Minatore" and that of "MasterNode". The former perform the same function performed for other cryptocurrencies, namely that of creating blocks and validating transactions that take place in the network. The "MasterNodes" have a different task, they are the ones who deal directly with the "optional functions" of

Dash. The optional functions are in fact additional services that, for a fee, can be requested by those who make transactions through Dash. There are two optional functions: the so-called "Private Send" and "Instant Send". The first function concerns precisely the possibility by the users of the Dash payment services, to carry out their transaction in complete anonymity.

This service takes place by "mixing" several transactions made by subjects who want to use this service. The mechanism consists of Dash's outgoings and revenues from one public address to another. Through this mechanism it will not be possible to trace in any way, who made the individual transactions, also in consideration of the fact that each user has 100 public addresses for each public key and a total of 100 public keys.

"Instant Send" consists of the possibility for those who hold a Wallet Dash to carry out transactions that are authenticated immediately (1.4 seconds on average). These two functions are, as mentioned, guaranteed by the MasterNodes; they are indeed particularly important "knots". The MasterNodes must be active 24 hours a day and 7 days a week, and to operate they must deposit at least 1000 Dash coins in the system.

The MasterNodes, in addition to the functions described above, have another important function. In fact, by virtue of the large amount of Dash they hold, they have the right to actively participate in the development decisions of the Dash network.

The development of the Dash network works through the financing of projects proposed by users or developers. These projects, which can be presented in a special section of the site, are analyzed and finally put to the vote of the MasterNodes. The projects chosen by the MasterNodes are financed by the network itself and thus allow to improve the functioning of the Dash network. Funding is self-financing as, projects are paid for through the Dash payment to programmers.

Self-financing takes place through a sort of "taxation" of the network, at the time of the creation of a block. When a block is created by miners, the amount of Dash generated by that block is distributed in this way: 45% of the Dash generated is attributed to the miner who solved the hash corresponding to the block, another 45% of the proceeds are distributed to the MasterNodes, as remuneration for the task performed to guarantee the optional functions, and the last 10% is deposited in the "Treasury".

The "Treasury" is a sort of "current account" of the Dash network itself, within which 10% of the Dash generated through the blockchain mechanism converges. The funds contained in the Treasury are spent on remunerating those who propose and develop projects that help improve the Dash network. As mentioned above, the projects are selected by the MasterNodes through a system of "direct democracy" where each MasterNode votes on every decision that must be taken by the network.

CHAPTER 3

INNOVATIVE CYRYPTOCURRENCIES

After analyzing the panorama of Alternative Coins, now we look at innovative cryptocurrencies, i.e. those that have a substantially new characteristic feature in their functioning, compared to Bitcoin. Among them, two of the most important cryptocurrencies can be identified; the first is Ripple and the second is IOTA.

Both are atypical cryptocurrencies, meaning that their fundamental characteristics are unusual and profoundly different from those of normal cryptocurrencies. Ripple stands out for being a centralized cryptocurrency, in the sense that the operation, security and authentication of transactions is managed by a company. IOTA, on the other hand, is profoundly innovative because it does not use the blockchain, but functions through the "Tangle".

RIPPLE

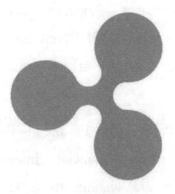

Ripple is a company, founded in 2012 by Ryan Fugger, based in California, that deals with the transfer of assets (understood as fiat currency, gold and other commodities), through its platform. The creation and development of the Ripple platform is the corporate purpose of the company in question and is pursued by the so-called "Ripple Lab" in San Francisco.

The Ripple company was created with the aim of developing a technology that It was designed so it could allow a new real-time payment system, and whose main function was to allow the transfer of funds between banks or financial companies. The company collaborates with a large number of banks, in particular European ones, and has developed a platform that was conceived as a competitor to SWIFT (Society For Wordwile Interbanck Financial Telecomunication) from which the term "SWIFT bank transfer" is used in technical jargon to mean an interbank and interstate payment.

Although it is only in the initial phase, the collaborations with financial intermediaries are numerous, and are leading to a feasibility study regarding the use of Ripple as a new platform for carrying out interbank transactions.

Another thing is the XRP cryptocurrency, commonly known as Ripple is an atypical digital currency, which many experts in the crypto world do not even consider a cryptocurrency. This foreclosure against XRP is mainly linked to the fact that the digital currency is not decentralized. Although it is based on the blockchain structure, it is controlled by the Ripple company, which develops and guarantees the transactions that take place within its platform.

Another peculiarity of Ripple, which distances it from the world of cryptocurrencies, is precisely the same goal with which it was created. Unlike most cryptocurrencies, XRP was not conceived as a commonly used "coin"; in fact, its function is that "money" that can be used between financial intermediaries, to allow the overcoming and efficiency of old technologies such as SWIFT.

This last feature of Ripple is perhaps the one that moves digital currency the farthest from the "crypto" world and the closest to the world of conventional finance. From this point of view, it can be said that XRP is the first point of conjunction between finance and the world of cryptocurrencies. In a context in which banks and financial institutions very often look to cryptocurrencies as a threat, and as a dangerous source of speculative bubbles, Ripple is the first among cryptocurrencies, that has managed to find concrete interest from financial intermediaries.

XRP has been released since 2012 by the same Ripple company. One of the fundamental characteristics of the cryptocurrency is that all the XRP units envisaged by the system were issued immediately; the expected amount of 100 billion units of XRP was "mined" at the time of the cryptocurrency's birth. The large amount of

Ripple mined (if you relate for example to the Bitcoin maximum limit of 21 million), was chosen precisely for reasons of functionality.

The value of Ripple cannot be as high as that of Bitcoin, because the creators did not want XRP to become a virtual store of value (virtual gold) as Bitcoin has become. But they envisioned it could be used in a practical way by Banks for the execution of interbank transactions. If the company's goal of replacing SWIFT technology was met, all banks would like to hold substantial amounts of XRP to sufficiently be able to secure the operations they want to carry out.

IOTA

IOTA is an open-source, non-mineable cryptocurrency project, developed and launched between 2015 and 2016 by a group of German developers. In support of the project, the "IOTA fondation" was founded with the contribution of funds donated by users.

IOTA is an innovative cryptocurrency born with a specific goal; to overcome the burden and heaviness of blockchain technology. As also stated on the official IOTA website, the developers wanted to operate in the direction of a "lightweight" cryptocurrency.

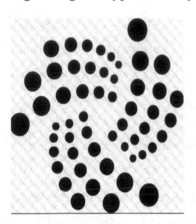

The inventors of the IOTA started from a very important assumption, namely that in the next decade it is estimated that there will be more than 50 billion devices connected to the Internet. These devices will be connected all over the world, even in countries where banking structures and financial services in general are almost absent.

In addition to the problem of the poor development of the financial economy, these

new countries that are facing the interconnected world, are characterized by inadequate state institutions, which fail to forcefully impose the state currency and which often subject it to strong devaluations. Such weak and highly depreciated coins prevent those who use it from making everyday payments. IOTA has the objective of allowing the management of "micropayments", guaranteeing their safety and having almost zero costs.

Interconnected devices will need to be able to exchange tiny amounts of money with each other, instantly. Precisely for this purpose, IOTA was conceived, which remains suitable for any other scenario in which there is the need to manage any type of transaction, even large ones.

To achieve this ambitious goal, at the time of designing IOTA, it was decided that it must distance itself from blockchain-based cryptocurrencies. While maintaining the vision linked to distributed consensus, a different approach was needed to make the network scalable within the IOTA ecosystem, where there will be tens of billions of connected devices. In fact, from the point of view of IOTA, we want to encourage the use of cryptocurrencies for everyday operations; doing so would have to validate thousands of transactions every second. As previously stated for other cryptocurrencies, including the expansion of blockchain blocks and the reduction of validation times, no cryptocurrency has so far been able to validate more than 200 transactions per second.

IOTA uses the Tangle, which is a software protocol based on direct acyclic graphs that are profoundly different from the blockchain protocol. Before proceeding with the explanation of the substantial innovation of the "Tangle", it is necessary to dwell on the concept of "direct acyclic graph". In computer science, and sometimes in mathematics, we mean by direct acyclic graph, also called "acyclic graph oriented "(from the English Directed Acyclic Graph, DAG), a particular category of graph direct or digraph.

The digraph is the more general structure of a simple tree chart. In a tree chart there is a common source and a set of nodes, positioned in multiple levels. The digraph, unlike the tree chart, does not have such an organized structure, but to each "source", nodes are not ordered in a regular manner. Inside the digraph there are "nodes", or "boxes" of the graph, and "arcs" or the path necessary to get from one node to another.

FEATURES OF IOTA:

No transaction costs: to send an IOTA transaction, the sender's device must verify two previous transactions in the Tangle, performing a "Proof of Work" operation. IOTA lacks the differentiation between "user" and "miner". All the subjects participating in the network are nodes of the IOTA network and must necessarily "work" to be able to participate.

Infinitely scalable: To send a transaction, two more must first be confirmed, and as the number of users increases, the efficiency of the network also increases. This way, the problem of other cryptocurrencies that allow a limited number of operations per second is overcome. The more the network grows, the more IOTA speeds up its transactions. The system adjusts to its size.

Quick transactions: The transaction execution times are inversely proportional to the number of transactions in the Tangle. When IOTA reaches mass adoption, transactions will be virtually instantaneous.

Fixed money supply: All existing units were created in the "genesis block", and that amount will never vary. The total amount corresponds to

2.779.530.283.277.761 iota.

CHAPTER 4

CRYPTOCURRENCIES 2.0

C ryptocurrencies 2.0, also known as "platform" cryptocurrencies, were born from an idea of Vitalik Buterim who is a Canadian programmer, of Russian descent. He is the inventor of Ethereum, which was designed in 2013 when he was just 20 years old. The idea of the Canadian programmer, was to exploit the 360-degree blockchain technology, not limiting its use to the application in the world of cryptocurrencies. Almost parallel to Buterim's idea, another similar operating platform developed, that of NEO.

The platforms are a development of web 3.0 in the sense that they aim to allow the widespread diffusion of the "Smart Economy", through the large-scale development of applications, shared software and smart contracts. The development of the Smart Economy in these platforms is favored by the opensource structure, and in general by the possibility of sharing information among all users. Each application and software can be downloaded for free by users and their scripts are "open" to any person who wants to consult them.

ETHEREUM

Ethereum, unlike Bitcoin, is not just a cryptocurrency; it is a decentralized platform for managing smart contracts. While Bitcoin is intended to serve as a virtual medium of exchange, Ethereum founder Vitalik Burerim did not want to limit his project to just this function. The concept of a platform is much broader than that of cryptocurrency. The Ethereum platform is also a cryptocurrency, the coin that runs in the Ethereum network is precisely the Ether (ETH in acronym), but its main feature is being a platform within which it is possible to develop applications, software and " Smart Contract ". The operation of

these contracts are embodied in the programming of applications that autonomously perform exactly what was programmed at the time of the agreement between the parties. This way there is no possibility of downtime, censorship, fraud or interference from third parties. Buterim's idea, when he started developing Ethereum in

2013, was to make the most of all the potential of the blockchain. In fact, he believed that the use of technology as a simple "ledger" for exchanging a cryptocurrency was limiting.

Development of Ethereum began in 2013 and the first version of the software became available starting in February 2014. Since then, a series of software versions have been made public that have introduced and developed three new programming languages for writing Smart Contracts.

To finance the development of the platform, Ether was launched for the first time in a public pre-sale offer, in a form similar to that of IPOs (initial public offerings), which made it possible to raise about $ 19 million in BTC.

In extreme simplicity, Ethereum could be presented as the largest shared computer that is capable of delivering enormous power available everywhere and forever. In other words, Ethereum is a computational platform that is "remunerated" through exchanges that are carried out through Ether. It is a platform that can be adopted by all those who wish to become part of the network and who in this way, will have a solution that allows all participants to have a shared and immutable archive. The Ethereum project is flexible and suitable for use in different application areas, it can be defined as a "Programmable Blockchain" that not only allows you to carry out predefined and standardized "operations", but allows users to create their own "operations".

The basis of the functioning of the entire Ethereum network is the platform's cryptocurrency, Ether. It is used for carrying out all transactions and operations within the platform. For example, a user who wants to "run" his own contract within Ethereum must pay for this service to the system in Ether. Similarly, a developer of an application or software through the platform must "pay" for the service offered by Ethereum. The payment may have either payments of Ether held by the subject, or through the subject's "work"; granting one's computational power to guarantee the Ethereum system.

With regards to the functioning of the Ethereum blockchain, it has the same characteristics as the Bitcoin one: a fundamental function is that performed by the "miners" who create the blocks and validate the transactions. A block is generated every 15 seconds on average, and as a reward for their work, miners receive 15 Ether per Block. The system has not foreseen a maximum number of Ether that can be emitted, for this reason there are currently around 100 million Ether in circulation. The number of Ether, according to what is currently foreseen by the system, will continue to increase constantly, according to the predetermined pattern. However, it cannot be ruled out that programmers may propose a change to the unlimited growth of Ether which, if accepted by the network, could lead to a gradual reduction of their emission, such as the example with Bitcoin.

SMART CONTRACT

The distinctive feature of Ethereum, as well as its most important innovation, is the introduction of "Smart Contracts". Smart contracts are computer protocols that facilitate, verify, or enforce, the negotiation of partial or total execution of a contract. In short, they are contracts that are executed automatically by a system. With contracts of this type, many types of contractual clauses can be made partially or fully automated, self-fulfilling, or both. Smart contracts aspire to ensure greater security than existing contracts and to reduce costs of the transaction associated with bargaining.

The Ethereum platform itself guarantees smart contracts, which is responsible for authorizing, validating and authenticating contracts.

NEO

NEO is the second most important blockchain platform after Ethereum; it is a Chinese developer project, launched shortly after Ethereum in February 2014, which aims to compete with the first platform.

NEO's ambitious goal is to help economic change through the development of the "Smart Economy". The NEO project manages smart contracts and software development on its platform by means of a payment with the platform's coin, the NEO. The platform works through a blockchain whose blocks are generated at intervals of 15 seconds each. The functioning of the network is always guaranteed by the miners, who create and authenticate in blocks and are therefore rewarded for their work with an amount of cryptocurrency.

The NEO programmers, while admitting the similarity of their project compared to the Ethereum one, identify an advantage in terms of scalability, (i.e. the number of operations that can be authenticated by their blockchain every second). An important difference with respect to Ethereum, is that NEO supports various computer languages in common use, such as Microsoft.net and Java. On the other hand, Ethereum requires specific knowledge of its programming languages. Another difference between the NEO and the Ethereum project lies in the quantity of NEO units that can be issued, the limit is set at 100 million units.

FIGURE 2.14119

NEO units are not divisible, in fact it is not possible to buy for example 0.5 NEO. The number of NEOs that can be held must always be an integer. For this reason, for operations within the network, the "GAS" is used as an exchange cryptocurrency, a cryptocurrency subordinate to NEO, but operating in the same network. Anyone who holds NEOs for a certain period of time in their portfolio they receive a quantity of GAS proportional to the amount of NEO held, as if it were a kind of "dividend". In this way, NEO holders have an incentive to hold the cryptocurrency for a long time.

ICO

The ICO (Initial Coin Offering), is a fundraiser through which a "Token" or a "Coin" is offered through a blockchain platform, in exchange for fiat currency or another cryptocurrency (such as Ether, NEO or Bitcoin).

ICOs take place within platforms such as Ethereum and NEO and are implemented through a Smart Contract.Here, a Smart Contract is generated so that the two counterparties are: the company or the person who wants to place the Token or Coin on the market; the person who intends to sign the ICO. Through this contract, the subscriber will receive the cryptocurrency placed on the market at the deadline set by the contract. The proceeds raised through the ICO are used to finance the business or project of those who launched the offer.

The financing mechanism through the ICOs is reminiscent of that carried out by companies that want to go public through the IPO (Initial Public Offering). While similar in scope, the ICO is profoundly different from the initial public offering. Firstly, cryptocurrencies are digital assets, but they do not specifically fall within a financial instrument that is clearly regulated by lawmakers. The parties who are listed to participate in an IPO are protected by the law and have the right not to purchase the newly issued shares until the day the share is actually listed. The most important thing to point out is that when those who participate in an IPO buy the shares of a company; they become shareholders.

The token or coin object of the ICOs can be exchanged and used like a normal cryptocurrency, but their operation and the authentication of their transactions takes place in the same blockchain as the platform on which they are launched.

Those who "launch" the ICO, referred to as "sponsors", usually provide access to a "white paper" describing the project, key team members, and key terms of the ICO (for example, the terms financial statements, contract details and timing).

In the underwriting process, the participant is typically required to transfer cryptocurrency or a fiat currency to one or more designated addresses or the ICO "sponsor" online wallet. Registrations can be completed in minutes. An entity can also be rewarded with ICO tokens by doing some tasks for the issuing company, such as marketing on cryptocurrency forums. Once the ICO is complete, the ICO tokens are distributed to the designated addresses or online wallets of the participants.

CHAPTER 5
INVESTMENTS IN
CRYPTOCURRENCIES

The main methods of investing in cryptocurrencies and methods of earning interest on them are briefly described below.

Trading - Through the use of regulated exchanges, it is possible to buy and exchange cryptocurrencies by approaching a global market, open 24 hours a day and 7 days a week. Users have mainly two types of exchange available: centralized (controlled by private companies, where the funds must be sent to the wallets of the exchange itself), and decentralized (the funds remain in the possession of the user and the trading takes place on peer to peer platforms).

The former offer a more similar approach to traditional trading sites, however users may be subject to restrictions based on their country of origin, and they are more prone to hacker attacks. The latter are technically more complex, aimed at an advanced type of user, but offer a greater level of security both in regards to the safeguarding of funds and privacy. Finally, there are other methods to obtain cryptocurrencies quickly, such as swap.

ICOs (Initial Coin Offerings)- They are a crowdfunding category dedicated to Utility Tokens, or cryptocurrencies that through their possession, give access to products or services of a particular company. In the past, subject to strong discussions, they have allowed users to increase the invested capital in a very short time. The increasing exposure of users to this type of offer (investments were sent directly to the teams, without any guarantees), have resulted in the launch of numerous ICO scams.

A greater awareness on the part of users has subsequently made ICOs evolve into IEOs (Initial Exchange Offerings). Briefly, IEOs are similar to ICOs but are managed by large exchanges, which in addition to managing the crowdfunding operation, take the place of users by verifying the legitimacy of the projects presented. Therefore a user who has confidence in the exchange, is more inclined to invest in a project.

STOs (Security Token Offerings) - Are a crowdfunding category dedicated to Security Tokens, or cryptocurrencies that represent real shares of a particular company. This type of offer began to be defined after the regulators expressed their opinion on certain ICOs, defining them as security and not utility. Unlike traditional initiatives, through an STO, it is possible to reach a worldwide audience, through the sale and subsequent trading on a market; which, unlike traditional ones, is open 24 hours a day and 7 days a week. It is worth following the evolution of this type of offer as it could represent the majority of the initiatives that will take place in the future.

Lending - Investors can earn interest on cryptocurrencies through loans. The most common type of lending refers to that of exchanges, where cryptocurrencies are "lent" to traders who request them (borrowers). Most platforms guarantee a 100% return of the loaned capital as well as interest. This type of investment, although aimed at an expert trading audience, is enjoying increasing success thanks to the possibility of earning ever higher interests.

CRYPTO STRATEGIES

Top 10 crypto strategy

This system starts from the assumption that in the Top 10 crypto market capitalization, there is always a "hard core" formed by bitcoin,Ethereum,Litecoin,Bitcoin Cash,Ripple and Dash, while the other positions are quite variable and are traded in turn by coins such as Monero,Iota,Cardano,Ethereum Classic,NEO and NEM.

For example, starting with a budget of $1,000, you have to buy $100 of each of the cryptocurrencies in the top ten.Be sure to check them monthly and cash out when you reach the established goals.

Accumulation Plan Strategy (CAP)

This system was originally applied by banks to investment funds, but it is perfectly replicable also in the world of cryptocurrencies. The basic assumptions of CAPs are the progressive accumulation of capital and the reduction in risk thanks to "dollar cost averaging". Applying it to cryptocurrencies, for example, it is necessary to purchase three different tokens, two perhaps already established, such as bitcoin and Ethereum, and one "emerging", as it can Stellar Lumen. You then decide which sums to invest and how often you have to check the portfolio to see the trend.

Cryptocurrency investment strategy by value

Among the medium / long-term strategies, the "by value" strategy also stands out, which partly resembles the previous one (CAP), but differs in terms of the choice of currencies to bet on.

In this case, cryptocurrencies must be chosen based on their future potential, influenced by values such as; a solid project (see EOS, Verge, Tron), low prices, community of users andthe introduction of any new technologies. Research and analysis on these factors will help you in choosing the right coins for the strategy.

Millesimal cryptocurrency strategy

This is a crypto investment strategy that is based on the analysis of the performance of those tokens that started from a few cents and have made a bang, reaching prices of hundreds of dollars.

We are talking about real "gold nuggets", and your task is to find them among the Top 100. It is advised to select at least five, invest 100 euros in each and keep the investment.

Crypto-trading strategy in the short term

After analyzing strategies indicated for the medium-long term, let's close this roundup with short-term crypto-trading. In this case, the goal is to speculate on the fluctuations that determine the price of an asset every day, or of a crypto in our case.

The strategy requires a lot of time and energy to follow the market, and is based on the simple concept of buying when the price goes down and selling when it goes up.

CHAPTER 6
WHAT ARE THE FIVE STEPS TO SUCCESSFULLY INVEST IN CRYPTOCURRENCIES?

1. Learn the basics

Don't invest in what you don't know! First understand the functioning of the blockchain, the terminology, the technical aspects and the dynamics that are involved in this world.

Don't be rushed, in-depth knowledge of a topic requires a long period of study.

2. Get experience

Crypto markets are quite young and subject to extreme volatility compared to traditional ones. Trading is not improvised and requires experience; you should always only risk an amount that you can afford to lose.

3. Follow the developments in the world of cryptocurrencies on a daily basis.

The world of Blockchain is running faster than any

other traditional sector, so keep up to date with its developments through news sites, social media and by participating in discussion groups on Telegram and other platforms.

4. DYOR - Do Your Own Research

Ensure that you do your research before investing in a project! Check all of the details of the cryptocurrency that you want to invest in, and ask yourself:

What is its capitalization?

What are the market volumes and what is the price history?

Are the people on the team real and verifiable?

Is the business registered according to law?

Is the project popular enough?

Does the whitepaper I am consulting reflect a specific mission, or do the objectives of the project seem unrealistic?

Is the team available to answer my questions and is the community following the project active?

Is the exchange I am using to trade safe and

registered according to the law? And when all this is not enough ...

5. Use your intuition

It's okay to be skeptical. If a project doesn't fully convince you, it may not be worth the investment. If you find that something is wrong or you are not confident enough, perhaps it is time to stop or exit the investment. Immobility is the enemy of a world in constant evolution, so try to inform yourself as much as possible and move in the market according to the knowledge you have acquired and your intuition.

Happy trading!

CONCLUSION

The objective of this guide was to verify the investment possibilities in a complex, non mature and constantly evolving market, such as that of cryptocurrencies. The analysis of the market and the "assets" that compose it was carried out by observing two guidelines. The first was to identify the relevant and distinctive characteristics of cryptocurrencies from a theoretical point of view. This was pursued by explaining the differences between the most important cryptocurrencies and cataloging them.

However, the difficulty of definition and the lack of legislation is not a matter of little interest. In fact, it has an important fiscal repercussion, just think of the taxes on capital gains that should be paid in the event that a cryptocurrency is considered a financial investment. In addition, it should be remembered that if cryptocurrencies were financial investments, considerable information and broader transparency should also be guaranteed, which at this time is not guaranteed at all.

In addition to tax considerations, it must be taken into account that the market of cryptocurrencies and "Blockchains" in general, is very young. The market is not only young but has until recently, been "dominated" in terms of market capitalization by a single "asset": Bitcoin.

To add to these problems, the strong impact that exchanges have on the price of cryptocurrencies, is substantiated in the request for high fees for commissions. This high incidence of commissions is a consequence of the risk to which operators who offer to mediate, in exchanges between fiat currencies and cryptocurrencies are exposed. Such a volatile and poorly regulated market, in fact forces intermediaries to protect themselves and request a profit proportional to the risk taken for the service performed. The situation outlined above is a symptom of non-total market liquidity.

In addition to this, it should be noted that the number of exchanges, although it has greatly increased in the last period, still remains low. The small number does not favor competition, which if it were tougher, would undoubtedly lead to a reduction in commissions.

BITCOIN AND CRYPTOCURRENCY TRADING FOR BEGINNERS 2021

Basic Definitions, Crypto Exchanges, Indicator, And Practical Trading Tips

Warren Larsen

Bitcoin and Cryptocurrency Trading For Beginners 2021:

Basic Definitions, Crypto Exchanges, Indicator, And Practical Trading Tips

Copyright © 2021 WARREN LARSEN

Written by WARREN LARSEN.

Errors and Feedback

Contact us if you find any errors

INTRODUCTION

In recent years, there has been a real revolution in the digital world: cryptocurrencies. The history of cryptocurrencies is relatively short, as the origins date back only to the second half of the 1990s. Already in 1998, what was called "B-Money" was published by Wi Dai: an anonymous and distributed electronic money system. Subsequently, Nick Szabo created "Bit Gold". Just like Bitcoin and other cryptocurrencies that would follow the technology, Bit Gold was an electronic cryptocurrency system that required users to complete the proof of work scheme. However, it was still the dawn of cryptocurrencies. In 2008, the first decentralized cryptocurrency was created: Bitcoin (ForexItalia24, 2017). Bitcoin is an online communication protocol that facilitates the use of a virtual currency, including electronic payments. Since its inception in 2009 by a group of anonymous developers known as Satoshi Nakamoto, Bitcoin has executed over 300 million transactions and has seen dramatic growth. This development has interested and subsequently attracted the attention of many people, becoming opportunities for huge profits. These are the conditions that made Bitcoin famous and that allowed the evolution of the entire system. Cryptocurrencies have further acquired a viral component by introducing a sort of "gold hunt" thanks to their diffusion in social networks and the most important media. There are many American companies that exploiting this virality, giving rise to a singular phenomenon. Many of these by changing their name, adding a term related to the world of cryptocurrencies to it, perceived an enormous growth in their listing on the stock exchange. Famous is the case of the American tea company which by transforming the company's name from "The Long Island Iced Tea" to "Long Blockchain Corp" perceived an instant growth of its shares equal to 200%.

Unlike the traditional stock market, this market is not yet regulated. There are no central entities or complicated financial systems, and the value of each currency is closely linked to supply and demand. This system has shown a high degree of volatility and non-stationary prices.

1.

WHAT IS BLOCKCHAIN?

T he blockchain, quite simply, is nothing more than a distributed database. From Wikipedia, we get an easy to understand definition of what a database is: "a data archive structured in order to rationalize the management and updating of information, and to allow the carrying out of complex searches." So, by translating this definition into a language that is easily understood by everyone, we are talking about a virtual space in which it is possible to store all kinds of information.

However, we have said that a blockchain is not simply a database, but a distributed database. This means that a copy of the information stored in this database is kept on each of the computers that are part of the network. But if a blockchain is nothing more than a database, what makes this technology so revolutionary? Simple, what makes this technology so innovative is the fact that unlike any other database, the

108

blockchain is substantially armored. Everyone knows that any IT infrastructure can be hacked, no matter how many security measures it may have. When a database is accessible through the web, it can be hacked.

We will understand better in the course of the next chapters why this infrastructure cannot be corrupted in any way; for now, let's just get familiar with the that is that a blockchain is basically a distributed and armored database. The fact, then, that this data archive is "distributed" allows us to begin to become familiar also with the concept of "decentralization." Normally, the databases are "centralized;" that is, they are owned by a company or an institution that takes care of updating them, making them accessible to people who may need to consult them, and putting in place all security measures necessary not only to prevent information theft, but also to prevent the data stored on that infrastructure from being manipulated and corrupted.

However, since we have said that the blockchain is a distributed database, we understand that there is no "central" body that deals with doing all these things, but that all the computers on the network collectively participate in these processes. Simplifying a bit, we can say that there are three types of networks: the "centralized networks" (often also called "stars") in which data is transmitted from a central point to all users, the "decentralized networks" in where we begin to have central nodes that transmit information between them without a precise hierarchy, and the "distributed networks," in which all the nodes are in communication with each other without there being a defined hierarchy.

Understanding these first concepts, we already have a way to understand why blockchain technology is commonly considered the greatest technological innovation after the advent of the internet, because for the first time we have at our disposal a perfectly secure database without the need for a central body to manage it and ensure its safety.

HOW BLOCKCHAIN WORKS

In the previous section, we explained that a blockchain is a distributed database. Here, we will try to explain how it works. To make it easier to understand everything, we need to give a concrete example of the most typical use case concerning this technology: the transfer of value (or money) from one user to another. To transfer money from one person to another, the method most of us are used to is wire transfers; what happens, very simply, is that each bank keeps registers in which it reports the total balance of each account holder and the movements made to and from that particular account.

When I make a transfer (let's say € 100) from my account to that of another person my bank tracks the movement and marks on its register a transaction for an amount equal to -€ 100 from my account, then scales this sum from my total balance and sends the money to the bank of the recipient.

This, in turn, will do the same by marking (but this time on its register) a movement of + € 100 and adding it to the total balance of the current account holder beneficiary of the transfer. Exactly the same thing happens with a blockchain, except that the register does not hold it by a bank but (as we have illustrated in the previous chapter.) Instead, all the computers participating in the network have a copy of this document; for example, when I send a Bitcoin (BTC) to a person, all the computers participating in the network mark the movement on the register and deduct 1 BTC from my account while, at the same time, add up the same amount for the benefit of the recipient. The first question that arises at this point concerns the fact that, since the register is not only shared by all the computers on the network but is also public (that is, it is accessible to everyone in consultation through special sites called "explorers"), anyone could have access to the handling of my account, thus damaging my privacy. In reality, the accounts (or "addresses") are not attributable to a name and a surname (i.e. to a natural person) but are "strings" consisting of a minimum of 26 to a maximum of 35 alphanumeric characters.

For this reason, bitcoin transactions are said to be anonymous. In reality, bitcoin is not anonymous, but "pseudo-anonymous." This means that although the addresses (those we call "current accounts" in the bank) are not registered in the name of real natural persons, it is still possible (though not easy) to follow the computer traces that these transactions leave on the web up to the user (i.e. the point where the user connected to the internet or the device with which he is connected) and thus define the identity of the natural person who controls that particular address.

Let's go back to our money transfer and introduce another relevant difference compared to what happens in the banking system; while when I move my money through a bank it immediately traces each transaction and does the same with any other movement, in a blockchain the operations made by the various users are "merged" and inserted into blocks. To understand what a block is, we can imagine it as a box that contains the information (sender address, amount handled, recipient address) relating to all transactions "ordered" by users in the unit of time. With Bitcoin, for example, a block is generated every 10 minutes.

Blockchains are very similar to taking inventory of physical goods. When we do an inventory, all we do is take all the goods we have in stock, put them inside some boxes (numbered in ascending order), recording the contents of each individual box on a register. By carefully ordering the different boxes, once the inventory is finished, we will also have a paper "map" that illustrates where each single item is located in the warehouse. If we imagine the inventory of a restaurant that is closing its business, for example, we find all the kitchen utensils (knives, cutlery, plates, pots, glasses, etc.), stored in a warehouse and placed inside boxes. Since the boxes are numbered and I have recorded the contents of each box in the register, whenever I need, for example, the colander, consulting the register I could know its exact location. A blockchain, therefore, can be thought of as the inventory of all transactions Made. In practice, it is nothing more than a huge register that records the trace of all the blocks executed by the network since its birth.

As you read this text, for example, the network is processing a new block and adds it to the register of all blocks processed over time. The term "blockchain" translated into Italian means in fact "chain of blocks" and gives a good idea of how this whole process works; each block registered on the blockchain is linked (like the link of a chain) to the previous one.

This aspect is fundamental to understand why this technology is so reliable. If an attacker tried to manipulate the information contained in one of the blocks already processed by the network, this

115

modification would cause a series of chain anomalies on all the blocks. The other computers on the network, finding themselves dealing with a document different from the one they had at their disposal, would be able to define the malevolent nature of the operation, thus blocking it instantly. The computers that are part of the network, however, do not limit themselves to transcribing the transactions present within a block on the blockchain; they also validate them. When the block is validated by the network it can no longer be modified. The blockchain, therefore, is not only an armored and distributed register (or database,) but it is also immutable.

Let's stop for a moment to summarize the concepts expressed up to now. When a user wants to transfer money to another user, what he does is send the sum from his address to that of the recipient. The information of this single transaction is entered inside a block together with the information relating to all the transactions ordered in the last ten minutes. The network then takes charge of the block, processes it, validates it, and transcribes it on the blockchain.

From that moment, the information contained in the block becomes immutable and can no longer be modified. Easy, right? Well, in the next we will illustrate how the network validates and processes the blocks, and we will have the opportunity to understand why the nodes that are part of this network cannot in any way manipulate the information contained in the block that they are processing. In other words, we will define who the miners are, what kind of role they have, and why they are so important in the functioning of a blockchain.

2.

WHAT ARE CRYPTOCURRENCIES?

After defining what a blockchain is, how it differs from DLT technology, how the validation process of a block works, and what some of the most common consensus protocols that represent the heart of any distributed database consist of, let's move on to more strictly than cryptocurrencies. However, we will try to do so not only from a purely technical point of view, but also from a philosophical point of view, questioning ourselves on concepts such as "value" and "money."

Let's establish that the definition of cryptocurrency is not something to be taken for granted; although Bitcoin has existed for ten years, and has given life to a real ecosystem around it, we have not yet been able to find a commonly shared definition of what a cryptocurrency is.

Just take a tour on the web to check how each of the protagonists of this world (the major developers, university professors, CEOs of companies operating in this sector, etc.) has had the opportunity over time to provide their own personal definition of this word, without the emergence of the one capable of making everyone agree.

Consequently, what I will do is provide my definition of what a cryptocurrency is, taking care however to warn the reader that what will follow is not teh singular definition of what cryptocurrencies are. Therefore, after a few years of reflection, I came to define a cryptocurrency as "a unit of data whose origin it is possible to establish with certainty, who owns it, and to which it is possible to attribute a value conventionally accepted by anyone."

To understand well what we are talking about, it will be necessary to give concrete examples; we have already mentioned how it is possible to follow every single BTC transaction through websites (explorers.) If we search for "explorer bitcoin" on Google, one of the first results is the "blockchain.com" site, which shows us a screen which lists the succession of the last validated blocks. Clicking on any block, therefore, we can view information such as the number of transactions it contains, the progressive number that identifies the block (i.e. the height of the block itself), and the total value of the transactions it contains.

What interests us to note is that each block has a weight, the maximum weight, but it would be better to speak of "maximum size." Generally speaking, a BTC block (just to give an example) is 1MB. Within each block, we find the data relating to each transaction. Among the data available to us, we have the block within which it was validated, the number of confirmations received, the timestamp, the weight, the size and much more.

Why am I writing all this? Because on the blockchain we go to archive data, and that data can be anything. It can be for example a medical record of a patient, the right of ownership in a car, or whatever else we can think of. Currently, if we take the example of BTC, the data we choose to record in the blockchain is transactions..

A blockchain, in other words, is nothing else a book that tells a story. More precisely, the story it tells is that of the chronological succession of all the transactions processed and validated by the network. If I wanted to create a register of registered cars using a blockchain to which a cryptocurrency was linked, I could easily do it today. In practice, we would have a coin that corresponds to the ownership of a specific car, and on that coin we would write all the car's data (make, model, year of registration, etc.) and the owner's data (year of purchase, purchase price, name, etc). The day in which the car was sold to a new owner, he would also receive the relative cryptocurrency on which his would be added.

What we need to do, therefore, is to stop imagining a cryptocurrency as a dollar bill, and start imagining it instead as a small box; in that small box you can put any type of information, and at that point you can also exchange the information with a third party and attribute a value to it. When we talk about BTC, each coin is like a small box that contains information, so the question at this point is: what is the information we are trading when we trade a BTC? The information we exchange is the most essential of all, the right of ownership over that box that we exchanged. When I send a Bitcoin from my address to another person's, the information that is stored on the blockchain is that that coin (not another, not any of those in circulation, but exactly that coin) ceases to be owned by my address and becomes the property of a new address. How can we be sure of the unique ownership of the coin? Because we have its private key. We will deal with this concept, and others equally important, in the following chapters.

3.

HISTORY OF BITCOIN

In the previous chapter, we had the opportunity to hint at how, over the years, Bitcoin has begun to build a sort of "standard" comparable to that of gold, so that every time the economy of a state begins to show signs of weakness we can see an increase in cryptocurrency trading volumes in that particular country. This is a trait that has characterized Bitcoin since its inception.

It was back in 2008 when an anonymous actor made his appearance, proposing a global currency supported by a P2P network in conjunction. In a sense, this was in response to the banking scandals that earned the honor of the news by following one after another and essentially representing the beginning of the great economic crisis that would infect the economies of the rest of the world. This person, whose true identity is still unknown over ten years later, will go down in history under the pseudonym of Satoshi Nakamoto.

More precisely, Satoshi makes his appearance in November 2008 by publishing on "The Cryptography mailing list" (on the site "Metzdowd.Com") a document concerning the consent protocol that will allow the operation of Bitcoin; a few months later, the first version of the software would be distributed and other developers start working on it. Just over a year after the birth of Bitcoin (in 2010) Satoshi withdraws from the community, his last public message dates back to 2011 and serves to communicate the handover with Gavin Andresen.

This is perhaps the strangest thing about this

technology, that the person who basically invented it was able not only to remain anonymous all this time, but even decided to completely exit the scene. Within less than two years after giving life to his creation, Satoshi Nakamoto vanished, but his legacy will live in every university course that disussed cryptocurrency and blockchains.

The important thing to understand, when we think of Satoshi, is that we are talking about one of the brightest minds of this century. The math that supports Bitcoin and allows it to work is commonly considered so advanced that many have come to argue that behind the pseudonym of Satoshi Nakamoto there is not a single person but a team of hackers with very solid skills.

In the Netflix documentary Banking on Bitcoin (2016) we can find one of the most plausible reconstructions of how things went. The creation of bitcoin should have been one of the major exponents of the cypherpunk movement, so inevitably one or more between Nick Szabo, Hal Finney, Adam Back and Wei Dai. The cypherpunk, which probably almost no one has ever heard of in our country, if not perhaps a few "enthusiasts", was a countercultural movement made up informally of people interested in privacy which aimed to achieve individual freedom through the use of encryption. The ideological approach that these groups have always had has been of a libertarian character, oscillating between social anarchism, anarcho-individualism and anarcho-capitalism.

Even today, in 2018, the anarchist component in the world of cryptocurrencies is clearly recognizable, despite the fact that in this world there are also large banks, national institutions, entrepreneurs, and ordinary people who in any way can be defined except anarchists. This technology, in any case, has its roots in a cultural humus (the anarchist one) which still represents the common thread through more than a decade of technological development. But let's go back to Satoshi's identity, "Banking on Bitcoin" reconstructs who it may be that seems to me (and many others) to be very likely; behind the pseudonym of Satoshi Nakamoto there would be Hal Finney (a leading exponent of cypherpunk made in the USA), who fell ill with ALS in 2011 and died in 2014 at the age of 58.

There was also a time when Australian entrepreneur Craig Steven Wright seemed to be the real Satoshi, but soon this too was discarded. Some might say at this point that obviously Satoshi has now disappeared, having become rich, will have converted all his Bitcoins into dollars and will be spending the rest of his days sipping Cuba libre in the Maldives; in reality, the addresses owned by Satoshi are known, and these addresses are blocked by hundreds of Bitcoins that have not been moved for years. This is what leads us to suspect that Satoshi may be Hal Finney himself (who passed away in 2014), because there was a moment, when Bitcoin prices went up to $20,000, in which even only 100BTC had reached a value of 2 million dollars (and more than 100BTC are blocked on Satoshi's addresses overall); the fact that all this money has been stuck on their respective addresses all these years without ever being moved suggests the idea that the owner of those Bitcoins (i.e. Satoshi) simply passed away.

Given that we will never know the true identity of Satoshi Nakamoto (whose gender is not even known for certain,) BTC already appears to have outlived its inventor; and all this despite having experienced very bloody moments in the course of its young life. As I write this text, for example, BTChas lost about 80% of its value compared to the last peaks of January 2018, and this leads many detractors to argue that its end has come. However, what the detractors do not say is that BTC has already dipped several times over the course of its history, showing each time that it has broad enough shoulders to come out stronger than before. The first major collapse in BTChistory was already in 2011 when, after a mad rush that in a few months swelled the price from $0.92 to the exorbitant figure of $32 per coin, Bitcoin prices collapsed again around $2. "Now it's over" the experts said, "Bitcoin is dead" the newspapers ruled; but things did not go like this. The following year (2012), BTC immediately offered the first signs of strength, returning to around $7. Already in mid-January, however, a new slap pushed it down by almost 40%; however, it seemed to be a trivial correction, since the summer of the same year, prices returned to close to $15. When it seemed that Bitcoin would never recover its historical peak of 2011, the price exploded again,

129

marking, in the spring of 2013, a new high close to $ 50. In the following months, BTC would resume its run with new highs close to $100, and would hit a high in April 2013, touching $270.

"Bitcoin is unstoppable, it will be worth thousands of dollars," the most enthusiastic said, but instead BTC returned down, only a few days after reaching the new high, reaching $67 in the same month of April. At this point, prices entered a lateral phase, remaining fairly stable around $120 until the end of the year when a new bull run started that dragged the price up to $1100. Wow! It is a pity that within a few weeks the price will return to plummet, this time settling at $500 and remaining in a kind of sideways for the next 18 months. Thus we arrive at 2014, another annus horribilis for our cryptocurrency which, in the meantime, has climbed to almost touch the $900 level.

The reaction of the markets to all this is, understandably, a kind of massacre, the price of BTC plunged again and stood at $400, where it remained stationary for another couple of years. We come therefore to more recent times, when finally in January

2017 BTC returned to break the $1000 wall and begin a race that would bring it, between December 2017 and January 2018, to touch the new all-time high around $20,000. Since that moment, BTC has re-entered a new bearish phase, reaching lows of around $3,000 and giving a new voice to the detractors who once again rushed to affirm that "this time is the very end"; who among the detractors and supporters will have the last word is still unclear.

4

EXCHANGE
CRYPTOCURRENCIES

With the birth of Bitcoin, the need arose to exchange the new cryptocurrency with fiat currency. From the beginning, those who wanted to understand what this new currency consisted of had only two ways to do it: either to get hold of some Bitcoin by mining it (which was initially much easier than it is today,) or by buying it from someone who already owned it.

Over time, some traders began to accept this new form of payment; they too needed to convert that profit made in BTC into legal tender currency. Even the most avid supporters, those who have kept their BTC longer, have also had the opportunity to spend them over time.

Today, spending our cryptocurrencies has become

extremely easy thanks to cards, which allow us to instantly convert our cryptocurrencies by withdrawing cash at any ATM, but we have come to this over time, through an evolution that has lasted years. As anyone can imagine, initially there was not even a real market as there is today; at the beginning, there was only BTC, and the simplest way to convert it into fiat currency was to physically exchange it for cash. Obviously, bartering was not a very rational way to manage it, so soon the first exchange platforms (exchanges) were born, which today allow us to easily exchange even large volumes of cryptocurrencies.

In the next section we will discuss how it is possible to exchange cryptocurrencies between individuals, about the platforms on the internet that allow you to do so, and about some particular sites that allow us to exchange even large amounts of cryptocurrencies with current currency, legally guaranteeing total security despite the fact that we find ourselves working with complete strangers. All this, ultimately, is part of what until now we have called the "cryptocurrency ecosystem," a layered and complex reality of services that allow users to manage their cryptocurrency, to exchange it and to use it to buy goods and services.

LOCALBITCOIN

If from the first moment, it seemed obvious that the easiest way to exchange cryptocurrencies was in person, and that to build a "market" of this type (therefore based on a sort of barter) it was necessary to resort to the web. The very success of the internet, not surprisingly, had also passed through all those services that allow the sale of goods or services between individuals.

With BTC, things went exactly like this; even today there is a site called Localbitcoins(online since 2012) which connects those who buy and those who sell cryptocurrencies locally. Through Localbitcoins (and other similar sites), however, supply and demand are limited to meeting; that is, they have a first approach, while the real currency exchange is managed in person, typically in cash. In large cities, it is not difficult to find someone who also wants to buy significant amounts of cryptocurrencies by paying for them with cash, but it is no less difficult to suffer scam attempts in this way. In fact, there are not a few people who, for having

134

exchanged their cryptocurrencies in this way, found themselves with thousand euros of counterfeit money.

When proceeding with this type of exchange, therefore, it is always preferable to have the due precautions and never take anything for granted; the risk of being scammed must always be considered. Although it may seem unsafe, this type of exchange is still very much in vogue today, especially since the job offer also moves through these channels. In fact, there are many people around the world who have cryptocurrency to spend and would like to invest it in their project.

Obviously, it is not common to find advertisements on these platforms to be a baker, but there are numerous ones related to translation jobs, the creation of websites and smartphone applications, as well as a very large number of job advertisements related to the blockchain (issue a token, create a smart contract, write articles for specialized sites, etc). All this testifies to the revolutionary door of this technology; around the blockchain was born much more than a simple market. A real economy was born with lots of jobs, university courses with secure professional outlets, and projects financed for millions of euros.

The existence of sites like Localbitcoins shows us how the "crypto-economy," contrary to what its detractors claim, is not based on nothing, but rests instead on concrete foundations and it is supported at different levels. It is frankly impossible to think that people who have already come into contact with this technology, who have understood how it works, and who already use it regularly can stop doing it in the next ten years, while it is not difficult to imagine that in a similar period of time more and more people may decide to start using any of the hundreds of cryptocurrencies currently available on the market.

THE ESCROWS

If in any big city in the world finding someone who wants to exchange cryptocurrencies is all in all quite simple, in small towns things are not as easy. Despite this I myself, who also live in a small town, was surprised to find a person less than 2km from me who wanted to sell 3BTC in 2016.

To be honest, that person was also the only one in the whole province, so it was clearly a coincidence that he was right near my house. To all this we must add that in many countries banks are, understandably, reluctant to favor the movement of money towards cryptocurrencies and tend to block incoming and outgoing transfers connected to the accounts of some large exchange platforms. So how can you exchange cryptocurrencies even for significant amounts through the internet, without risking taking the proverbial package? Simple, we use special services called "escrow". On the internet, there are dozens of sites that allow you to do exactly this; the system is as simple as it is ingenious.

These sites are nothing more than a catalog of third parties who take on the responsibility of managing the transaction on behalf of all the parties involved; each of these users has a rating and requires a fee to carry out such a delicate task. The commission required by each escrow varies according to the rating that the user has accumulated, as the rating reflects the user's reliability.

With this system, therefore, scams become extremely rare and difficult. Escrows tend not to act in bad faith, since they are paid for their reliability, and their reputation is their livelihood. This system, of course, is not exactly the cheapest of all, and probably not even the most comfortable way to exchange fiat currency for cryptocurrencies. However, it has been used by thousands of users who have testified to its quality and effectiveness for years.

EXCHANGE PLATFORMS

There are many reasons why you may want to trade cryptocurrencies (with other cryptocurrencies or with fiat currency,) and there are also many different ways to do it; what we need to make clear is that there is a right way to satisfy every different need. Not understanding this simple thing, when dealing with cryptocurrencies, can lead to unpleasant inconveniences; a very common mistake, for example, is that the function of an exchange platform (or exchange if you prefer) is to allow the conversion of different cryptocurrencies into other currencies or fiat currency.

In reality, this type of service was created to allow trading and not to simply allow you to change your currencies. For example, imagine a lawyer who agrees to be paid also in cryptocurrency; since only a few clients decide to pay him this way, the lawyer tends not to spend that money and eventually accumulates a tidy sum on his BTC address.

At some point, our lawyer will want to spend this sum, and perhaps instead of spending his coins as they are he decides that the time has come to convert them into euros; what is the most comfortable way to do it? Well, just open an account on one of the largest and most reliable trading platforms on the market and transfer the BTCs to their address, at which point you place a sell order in euros and that's it, right? Well, things won't necessarily turn out to be that simple. The moment our lawyer tries to transfer the sum just converted into euros to his current account, the account could be frozen, simply because he didn't read the compliance policy.

Obviously not all exchanges adhere to this type of protocol. It simply depends on the different rules that different countries apply to manage this type of market. In Italy, for example, opening an exchange requires compliance with very stringent rules and is therefore not a simple (and even less economical) activity to start.

This set of rules (compliance,) provides, among other

things, the identification of users (which is why today almost all platforms require the sending of user documents) and that the funds deposited are used specifically for trading. Our lawyer was wrong in thinking he could just exchange his BTC. Since his behavior is considered improper and expressly prohibited by the regulation of the platform, our lawyer found his account frozen.

This does not mean that it is not possible to use an exchange platform to change our BTC?That of the lawyer is just one example of the risks that a lazy person takes when not doing things with due attention, but there are numerous exchanges on the market, even among the largest, which do not have such strict rules.

The world of cryptocurrencies is refractory to the regulations imposed from above, hence the fact that users (including traders themselves) are forced to sacrifice their privacy in order to legitimately operate with their coins (since they have to submit their documents to exchange platforms to open an account.) It's not exactly one of the most popular norms within the community; at a certain point, users on social networks, forums, and blogs began to tell each other that it would not be a bad idea to build a decentralized exchange.

After all, what else is an exchange platform but an updated register of all the exchanges made? Exactly the type of data that can be processed through a blockchain, as long as there is a decentralized network of nodes that guarantees its functioning. At this point anyone can guess why at this very moment on the market there are at least a dozen platforms (with related native cryptocurrencies in tow) that offer exactly this service; users can transfer their coins to these platforms and do their own trading (or just simply change their coins) just like they currently do with large centralized exchanges. Where is the difference? That in this way they can do it anonymously and, in many cases, without paying commissions for every operation they make.

A recent innovation has also contributed to making this even easier to achieve, known as the "atomic swap," which allows users to use a smart contract to process an exchange of currencies between coins belonging to different chains. In this exchange, the smart contract essentially acts as a real escrow (thus protecting both parties involved,) making sure to send the coins to the relevant valid addresses. Let's imagine that a user wants to buy ETH using their BTC; a smart contract will take its BTC, it will search for one or more users capable of satisfying the request at the price set by the user, and as soon as this is possible it will self-execute by paying the respective parts to the addresses that each of them will have previously established.

Decentralized exchanges are one of the best examples of the advantages of disintermediation which, inevitably, also coincides with a drop in the costs incurred by the end user. The reduction of costs, then, becomes an extraordinary incentive to convince more and more users to abandon centralized models in favor of decentralized ones and that is why, at least in the long term, all this new technology based on disintermediation and decentralization seems inexorably destined to win over the (centralized) models that currently regulate some of the main aspects of our social life.

5.

INTRODUCTION TO
CRYPTOCURRENCY TRADING

Inserting a chapter dedicated to trading in a text that deals with blockchain and cryptocurrencies is inevitable; one of the advantages of this technology is that all those who discover it immediately feel the need to begin to understand how the market works. The reasons that push a person to start trading cryptocurrencies can vary. There are those who do it out of pure curiosity, to better understand the same technology, or simply because they see the possibility of earning money. In any case, it is extremely common that those who approach cryptocurrencies very often decide to open a trading account on an exchange platform.

This has allowed many people to acquire the first rudiments of economic-financial education: a form of education that is almost completely absent in our country and which would be greatly needed. The "quantum" leap that people who start using BTC and other cryptocurrencies make is that since they have full control of their money, they can also freely invest it. And for the rest, as I like to say, "Even a monkey can make a profit by trading." What does this activity consist of? I think one word is enough to say it and that word is "rules." Trading is a system of rules.

What a trader does is take advantage of these value fluctuations to make a profit, buy BTC at a low price (for example at $100) and resell at a higher price (for example at $120); the difference between the selling price and the buying price represents the profit (or loss) realized with that single operation.

In cryptocurrency trading, we can observe two big trends: that of traders who always operate in pairs with a fiat currency (for example, they buy BTC to earn dollars,) and those who trade in cryptocurrencies (they buy any altcoin to earn BTC.) Whoever operates in the first way (i.e. accumulates dollars) is a person who is probably convinced that the supremacy of fiat currencies will never be scratched by cryptocurrencies, and consequently uses price changes to earn more legal tender currency. Those who instead operates in the second way (i.e. accumulates Bitcoin) is convinced that, regardless of what happens during bearish cycles, BTC is destined in the long term to continue to increase its value, always hitting new peaks.

The most popular trading strategies include:

1. Scalping: means that the trader opens and closes numerous transactions during the same day, aiming to make a profit in the shortest possible time by taking advantage of even the smallest price changes.

2. Day trading: in this case the trader tends to make fewer operations, rarely exceeding two or three in the

same day, and as a basic rule each operation is opened and closed strictly within 24 hours.

3. Swing trading: those who do this type of trading reduce the number of transactions even more compared to the day trader, and as a basic rule the duration of the trade is extended from one day (maximum duration of day trading) up to ten days (indicatively the maximum time frame within which the single transaction should be closed.)

4. Cassettista: operates more according to an investment logic than (as in other cases) in a purely speculative logic. Between when the drawer opens an operation and when he closes it, months can easily pass; moreover, it is difficult for this type of operator to manage more than two or three investments at the same time.

In general, a good trader knows how to adapt his operations to all four trading styles based on the market trend; therefore depending on the moment the trader decides to adopt one style instead of another, the same trader who today does scalping could then suddenly adopt a swing trading logic, and then go back to scalping

146

once the previous operations are closed.

As we said, trading is basically a system of rules, once these rules are set correctly you inevitably start making a profit; this does not mean that you will easily become a billionaire, but simply that you will be able to make your savings relatively easily. The difficult thing, when we talk about trading, is not even learning the technique (which after all is accessible to anyone), but having a full control of one's psychology.

Each trader is constantly exposed to a great psychological pressure that induces him, regardless of the rules he has given himself, to sell or buy in an unreasonable way; the point is that no matter how good you are, all traders are trading at a loss. A good trader simply accumulates more profit than loss. The psychological reactions of each operator can be different and can change, as well as from person to person, from situation to situation; therefore there are no rules valid for everyone to manage the most demanding aspect (which is the psychological dimension) of the trading activity.

In the next chapters, therefore, in addition to

describing the functioning of some fundamental tools in the activity of each trader, we will also try to make more general reflections on this type of profession to offer each reader a broad point of view and a sufficient basis.

HOW TO READ THE GRAPHS

Finding yourself trading when you discover cryptocurrencies is a very common thing, and the fact that those who approach this type of activity do so thinking of becoming immensely rich in record time is, unfortunately, the same. Even if anyone can learn to exploit the market cycles to profit, it is not certain that all those who engage in this activity will reach the goal. As mentioned before, trading is a system of rules, but since we impose these rules on ourselves, many tend to infringe on them. In any case, the first rule that every trader must follow is "never invest more than you are willing to lose."

The first thing we must do is to learn to read stock market charts which, in jargon, are called "Japanese candlestick charts." Obviously the price trend can also be graphically rendered by a line graph, but the candlestick charts give us much more information than we could obtain by observing a line.

The reason why these graphs are called this is quite intuitive: the graphic signs (those colored red and green) resemble candles. Each candle on the chart expresses the price trend in the unit of time defined by the user. Precisely for this reason we hear about charts for one hour, four hours, one day, one week, and so on; this is the length of time covered by one candle.

Now, let's imagine reading a 1D (one day) chart; we know that each candle graphically represents what happened over the last 24h. Therefore, if the candle is colored red this means that in the twenty-four hours the price has dropped, on the contrary if the candle is colored green it means that the price has gone up.

The height of the candle represents the chane in unit price. When we read a red candle (which signals a price drop in the unit of time) the upper border indicates the opening price, and the lower one the closing price of the session, and vice versa for a green candle.

In some cases, we can observe candles that are not colored and substantially resemble crosses. This type of candle indicates that the opening price was substantially

149

identical to the closing price; the edges of these crosses (directed upwards or downwards) graphically represent the price changes (maximum and minimum) that occurred during the session.

Let's take some practical examples and imagine that the price of 1BTC after starting from a price of $10 at the opening touched a maximum of $15 and then closed the session at $12. How is all this represented by the candle? Simple, in the meantime we will have a green candle (because the price has risen), similar to a rectangle whose lower edge is positioned at $10 (the opening) and the upper margin is positioned at $12 (the close); from the upper margin. Then, we will see starting a straight line ("shadow") that reaches $15.

As another example, let's imagine that the opening price is $20 and the closing price is $17, with the day's low at $15 and the day's high at $22; in this case the candle will be red (session at a loss), the upper margin (opening price) will be positioned at $20, from here the upper shadow (the straight line) will start, which represents the high of the day and will touch share $22, while the lower margin of the candle (closing price) will settle at $17, the level from which the lower shadow (always another straight line) will start and will reach the low of the day at $15.

For the last example, a session that opens and closes at $17, corresponding to the minimum of the day and with a maximum peak reached of $20. In this case the candle will look like a cross; it will not have any color because the opening and closing price coincide, and there will be no lower shadow because the day's low has never gone below the opening, but there will be a long upper shadow that it will extend up to $20.

Everything that we have illustrated in words up to now can be found summarized in the image below that will allow you to better understand all the new terminology we have introduced.

THE TECHNICAL ANALYSIS

In these few chapters we have discussed several fundamental concepts for trading, how to read a candlestick chart, and established that trading means creating your own system of rules. This last aspect is fundamental, because without an effective system of rules, we will never be able to trade effectively.

The purpose of these rules is not just to allow you to make a profit, but rather to allow the trader to ease the psychological pressure to which he will inevitably be exposed until the moment he closes the operation, and to establish instead how to realize the profit each operator is based on what is essentially a real "collection of signals".

The first question that every person inevitably asks themselves when they start trading is "what moves the price of a cryptocurrency?" Finding a good answer to this question already means you have taken the first step to becoming a good trader. The price is mainly driven by two factors: the greed of the market and the news breaking into the market. These two factors, taken together, generate the price movements that allow us to make a profit.

When we begin to operate on a particular market, any news concerning it can trigger a bullish or bearish reaction in the price trend. There is news, such as the possibility of a hard fork or the release of a new version of the platform, which inevitably trigger the rise in prices. Other news, however, can do the exact opposite and sink the value of a coin. For example, the price of a crypto may fall if the news spreads that the official wallet of a certain currency is defective or that a certain cryptocurrency is about to be excluded (delisted) from a large platform.

If understanding how and why news moves the market is easy enough, it is more difficult to understand the way in which the greed of operators causes price fluctuations. First of all, what we have to understand is that the price trend is never linear, but more resembles the waves as seen in the above candle charts.

When we begin to imagine the price trend as if it were a wave, we begin to frame two different trends: one short-term in which the price moves between minimums and maximums within what is called a "channel," and at the same time we find a second trend in progress, more in the long term, which sees the price destined to increase or decrease.

There are obviously several tools available to traders to recognize these trends in the price (some of which we will get to know later,) but in principle the dynamics we are witnessing are always the same. Since all traders pursue the same goal (making a profit) and all read the same chart at the same time, when certain conditions occur all traders will click en masse to take advantage of the opportunity and here, as mentioned, greed of the market ends up moving the price.

However, this is also true on the contrary; the fears of the market can cause a wave of sales that can lead the individual trader to suffer significant losses. The ability to read the market trends through the price trend on a chart, and to recognize the moments of reversal (both short and long term) in the main trend, is all classified as "technical analysis." What the trader does, in other words, is to use the tools at his disposal to define the trend of the trend and try to make a profit on the basis of technical analysis.

The bad thing about technical analysis is that it is not an exact science, but more of a statistical calculation. None of the data we get from reading the charts ever gives us guarantees; although there are more relevant (and more reliable) signals than others, there are no 100% safe trading signals. Moreover, every good trader naturally oscillates between a speculative approach and a more moderate one based on investment. Consequently, for a complete operation on the market, technical analysis is not sufficient, but it is always necessary.

All the concepts we are exposing exist on every type of market; the graphs read the same way both on the forex and the cryptocurrency market, the technical analysis is the same whether you are investing in stocks or buying coins, and fundamental analysis is a concept that always exists.

When we buy shares, for example, the fundamental analysis consists in reading the financial statements of the company we are going to invest in; in the cryptocurrency market, the fundamental analysis is done by collecting information of a different nature, as we will see better in one of the next chapters. For now, let's focus on knowing some elementary tools that every trader normally uses in his daily practice to search for trading signals that allow him to make a profit.

SUPPORTS AND RESISTANCES

We have said that the price moves like a wave within a long-term trend that can be bullish or bearish ; quite simply in a bull market the price tends to always touch new peaks, while in a bear market it tends to always touch new lows.

When in the middle of a well-defined trend, the price fails to touch a new peak (minimum or maximum.) This is a first sign of a weakening of the trend, and indicates that we may be close to a reversal of the main trend.

If we then graphically combine the maximum peaks reached by the price with a straight line, and do the same for the minimum peaks, we graphically obtain important levels at the level of technical analysis; these are called support (the line that joins the minimum peaks) and resistance (the line that joins the maximum peaks.)

Therefore, when the price is near a support, this represents a difficult level to break downwards, and it is easy to say that (in the short-term trend) the price is going to rebound. In the same way, when the price is near the resistance, is easy for the price to begin to slide down, seeking the first useful support again. However, we must always consider that the more times these levels are tested, the less likely it becomes that they can withstand the next wave. When the price starts beating against a resistance, sooner or later it is likely to be able to break it and therefore start to rise.

In this dynamic, there are two relevant moments for a trader's activity: when the price is near those price levels that we have called supports and resistances, and when the price breaks these levels. Given that today there are financial instruments that allow you to make a profit even when the price is falling (short sale), it would be preferable for a novice trader to concentrate on making all upward operations and then later to integrate more advanced tools into their operations.

Our neophyte cryptotrader, who wants to make a profit with the upward variations in the price, has two ideal moments to open a position: precisely when the price is near a support and when the price breaks a resistance. Opening a position by counting on the rebound near the support is a strategy that often allows you to make a profit, but which presents greater risks since it is not said that the support will hold. Instead, opening the position when the resistance is broken upwards is a more moderate trading strategy which allows us to take fewer risks but offers us less profit opportunities.

In any case, despite how sophisticated our market analysis skills are, no one can really predict where the price is going. This is always true, even more so in a market like cryptocurrencies, subject to continuous manipulation. In fact, as the cryptocurrency market is often not very liquid, some operators with large financial capacities are in a position to be able to provoke speculative maneuvers that are referred to as "pump and dump." They accumulate large quantities of coins at a certain price for weeks, and then suddenly inject enormous volumes of liquidity, causing a rise in prices that it will subsequently allow to resell to other operators at a profit.

After completing the speculative maneuver and painfully trimming the package to all the operators who had rushed to chase that sudden rise, the price of the currency (lacking the liquidity that had allowed the rise) falls back down.

Therefore, among the rules that should be given

when trading cryptocurrencies, we have that of not operating on illiquid pairs (which generate a trading volume lower than a minimum that is commonly established around 20BTC per day) and that of investing on projects that you know well and in which you have great confidence (so you have to study the various platforms, carry out your fundamental analysis and carefully choose which ones you want to operate on.) Before moving on, let's use a simple image to fix what we just said; in the following chart, we clearly see that the price moves within a "channel" limited by two lines that respectively join the minimum peaks (the red support line, and the black resistance line.)

When at a certain point the price shows a first sign of weakness and does not show itself capable of going to test the resistance again (black line) here it tries to breathe for some time near the support; at this point, we witness a last attempt at a bullish sortie, then the price suddenly drops, breaks the level (already tested several times previously,) crosses the red line (the support,) and enters a markedly bearish cycle in which at each new low one that is always lower than the previous one follows.

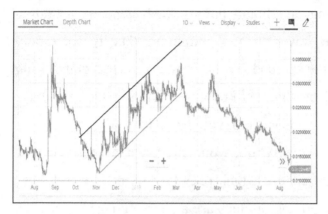

RELATIVE STRENGTH INDEX (RSI)

We have said that every trader uses, in his daily operations, a series of tools that help him to analyze the chart he is reading. These instruments can be divided into two broad categories: indicators (which freely replicate the price trend on the chart) and oscillators (which move in a pre-determined range of values.) These tools often give us very clear signals of what is happening to the price, and their correct interpretation is often what makes the difference between loss and profit.

The trading signals do not only come from reading the data we get from the indicators and oscillators, but also directly through the price chart by plotting ourselves the levels that represent the "supports" and "resistances." Since for each currency pair on which we operate we can change the unit of time (represented graphically by the candles,) we have a multiplicity of different signals depending on how we set the time frame. For example, if we are trading on the BTC-ETH pair, spending BTC to buy ETH.

Regardless of the modality we use to obtain the trading signal, in the meantime we must always start from the assumption that the signal is all the more solid the more the TF is set in an expanded manner; a chart with a one-week time frame, therefore, offers more solid signals than a chart with a one-hour time frame.

If I wanted to buy ETH spending BTC, what I would do would be to wait for a moment when a trading signal appears on the 1W chart, start observing the lower TF, then slowly narrow down the TF to find the optimal time to buy. To reduce the risk, therefore, we never rely on a single trading signal, but we go in search of what is called "convergence" of signals. If it is true that "many clues do not prove," it is also true that the more clues you have, the higher the chances of winning your bet.

Because in a sense this is what we are doing; we are betting that the price will go up. Among all the tools used by traders, is there one that is simple to understand and that is commonly used and appreciated by the majority of the community? Yes, it's called RSI (relative strength index.)

It is an oscillator that moves continuously between a minimum (equal to zero) and a maximum (equal to 100) invented by John Welles Wilder (who illustrated its operation to the public in 1979 with the book "New Concepts in Technical Trading System") and whose purpose is to help the trader identify the points where the strength of the trend is running out; the mathematical formula would help us understand why certain indications are obtained from the RSI. In any case, this does not change the operation, so let's just say that the RSI, moving between a minimum of zero and a maximum of one hundred, reaches two bands in which the trader's attention increases: the 0-30 band (which is defined as oversold) and the 70-100 band (which is defined as overbought).

When the RSI crosses the oversold and overbought

ranges, it means that the market is in a phase of "excess," in which traders are essentially stubborn to sell and buying beyond reasonable. Unfortunately, to make a profit, it is not enough to rush to buy in the oversold ranges and sell in the overbought ranges, based on the strength of the current trend. The RSI can remain in "extreme" conditions (oversold or overbought) for long periods of time.

There are particular moments, however, in which anomalies are produced on the RSI if we compare the trend of the oscillator with what we read on the price chart. For example, when we see the price mark a low of $20, rise up to $23, and then return to mark a new low of $17, what we clearly read on the price chart is that by combining the two lows we obtain a descending line. In certain circumstances, however, it happens that in conjunction with the two lows on the price chart, the RSI marks two peaks which, once joined, form an ascending line (which moves upwards.)

This kind of anomaly is called "divergence," and is formed not only on the RSI but also on other types of oscillators and indicators (always in the same way.)

There are basically two types of divergences: the bullish ones (which can be read by drawing a line that connects the minimum peaks) and the bearish ones (which can be read by drawing a line that connects the maximum peaks.)

Any kind of divergence we should notice between what we read on the price chart and what is expressed by the oscillator gives us a trading signal. In particular, if in a bull market we notice a divergence in the maximum peaks, we have a sell signal (there is therefore the possibility of a trend reversal.) If instead it is produced by combining the minimum peaks we have a buy signal.

More technically, we should then distinguish the actual divergences (two increasing peaks in the direction of the trend on the price chart in conjunction with two peaks in the opposite direction to that of the trend traced by the oscillator) from the hidden ones (in which the logic is reversed so the peaks expressed by the price are in the opposite direction to that of the trend, while the oscillator behaves in the opposite way.) In the following graph, however, we will analyze only the classic divergences, while we will deal better with hidden divergences in the paragraph dedicated to MACD. The RSI, in principle, offers us the best trading signals through the divergences that occur in the vicinity of the oversold and overbought ranges; such signals are more solid when they emerge on larger TFs.

A bullish divergence, for example, built on a chart with a one-week TF in a strong oversold situation and near solid support, is almost always a good time to open a long position. The more signals we have that push us to buy, the more naturally we will be prepared to open a position. To simplify all this reasoning, below we graphically illustrate the functioning of two classic divergences (the first bullish and the second bearish); what we see in the green box is that the price on the chart marks three new consecutive lows while the RSI at those lows is rising (all of this is graphically expressed by the red line.)

As soon as the price breaks, the resistance begins to grow and undergo an increase of about 30%. Immediately after, however, in the black box, we notice that a bearish divergence is formed. On the chart, the price marks two new highs, but the line that joins the respective peaks on the RSI (highlighted in red) is clearly descending.

This time, the support is broken and the price starts to fall. In a trader's operations, the orange circles represent the moment in which it would have been advisable to open the position (the first two) and close it (the last two) to optimize profit and reduce any risks. This type of strategy is not infallible, so by working exclusively with the divergences produced by the RSI we will inevitably end up even getting into some bad situations.

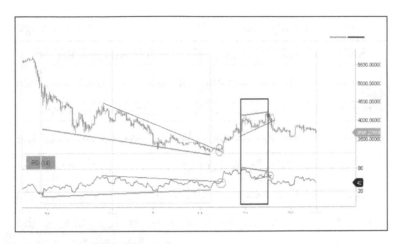

MOBILE MEDIA

What we must always have in mind when trading is that each chart offers us all kinds of signals, and it is up to us to interpret them correctly by making the different evaluations of the case. When we collect a signal using the RSI, we should go in search of confirmations using different tools to make sure that these also provide us with positive indications.

We have among the most useful and simplest tools to integrate into everyday operations moving averages; these tools only reduce the effect of random peaks by expressing the price trend on the chart in the form of a curve.

There are different types of moving averages; the

167

most commonly used are called simple moving average (SMA or arithmetic average) which assigns the same importance to all the values that the price assumes regardless of whether they are more or less recent, weighted moving average (WMA) which resolves the limit of the SMA by assigning greater relevance to more recent candles , exponential moving average (EMA) which assigns an exponentially increasing value to the most recent price values, and adaptive moving average, which introduces the analysis of volumes in the calculation necessary to produce the curve that expresses the price trend. Regardless of the type of moving average, the curve that will be represented by the graph will have different appearance depending on the "period" that we will have set; a 12-period moving average, for example, indicates that each point plotted by the curve represents the average of the last 12 candles.

Moving averages are therefore defined as "fast" and "slow" as the reference period increases. In this way, a 12 period moving average (based on the last 12 candles) is considered a fast moving average and a 26 period average (based on the last 26 candles) is considered slow.

Moving averages are important precisely because we can create multiple moving averages with different periods by receiving different indications; in general, the periods most commonly used in technical analysis to plot moving averages are 20-50-100, especially as regards the exponential moving average (which is the one that traders normally use the most.) These tools offer us a quick and immediate glance on the market; when the price is above a moving average the trend is for example considered bullish (on the contrary if it is below it is considered bearish.) The trend is also considered as the more marked the higher the period of the moving average above which the price stands.

This is because the moving averages also represent values of supports and resistances; the more solid, the greater the period used to build the moving average itself. Another very useful indication that the moving averages gives us is the way they intertwine, which tells us a lot about the future course of the trend. Normally when a faster moving average trims up a slower moving average, that is the time to buy; on the contrary, the cut down is the time to sell.

Let's try to observe everything we said on a chart (precisely a 1D chart of the BTC/XRP pair.) Here we have plotted three exponential moving averages at 20 periods (red curve,) 50 periods (blue curve,) and 100 periods (black curve) and highlighted (in green and black) two particular moments in the history of the price trend. Let's look at the first green rectangle; here at a certain point we clearly see the fast moving average (the 20-period one, colored red) cutting up the two slower moving averages. The price immediately falls back, uses one of the slower moving averages as support, and enters a markedly bullish cycle. In the second green box, we see the same dynamics with the price that first marks a big rise and then uses the slower moving average as support and returns to test the same resistance it had tested with the first rise. The development of the situation that we see unfolding in the green box is that either the price will break the short-term resistance (orange line) to then go and test the long-term one again (yellow line) or it will break the three supports represented by the three moving averages and it will fall back into the area of the last low (purple line) where in all likelihood it will either attempt a rebound or begin to build a divergence.

In the black squares we observe the same dynamics, but in reverse; in the first black box we can

observe how the fast moving average cuts down the two slower moving averages one after the other with the price that once passed below it will begin to test the EMA100 (exponential moving average at 100 periods, the black curve in our chart) exactly as if it were a resistance.

In the second black box, the same scenario is repeated but with less vigor; the price seems to be trying to gather around the moving averages but in the end the bearish cycle prevails and the price touches its minimum peak. Moving averages in general and exponential averages in particular are extremely useful in traders' operations, and if integrated into a broader strategy, they provide us with important indications on the possible future trend of the price.

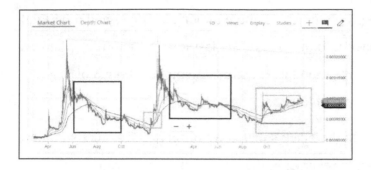

MACD

In the previous chapters, we started introducing the use of tools that should never be missing in a trader's toolbox. This small overview will cover another key tool, the MACD ("Moving Average Convergence / Divergence.")

The MACD is an indicator considered extremely useful by many traders, who usually integrate it into their operations, built substantially on the basis of data extracted from three different exponential moving averages (at 9, 12 and 26 periods.) One of the main uses of the MACD is to trace differences. Since in the last chapter dedicated to the RSI we dealt with the classic divergences, in this paragraph we will deal specifically with "hidden" divergence. The dynamics with which the divergence is constructed is the same as we have seen previously, so also this time by joining the maximum (or minimum) peaks plotted on the price graph with a straight line, we will notice anomalies (the divergences in fact) with respect to what we notice by tracing lines that instead join the peaks constructed by the MACD. The MACD is useful to us because it allows us to obtain more information on the solidity of the trading signal, when in fact we notice the same divergence both on the RSI and on the MACD. This is to be understood as an additional proof of the validity of the signal; the MACD then gives us another interesting starting point, being in fact graphically represented by the trend of two curves, which are substantially two different exponential moving averages (EMA) normally highlighted with blue or black colors (for the slower moving average, at 26 periods) and with red color (for the fastest moving average,

Therefore, when the faster moving average cuts up, the slower one we have a bullish signal, and when the slower moving average is cut down by the faster, one we have a bearish signal. In any case, as we have done

173

in the other paragraphs, we use an image to fix the main concepts.

This time we took two photographs of the market, highlighting them with rectangles (green and black); in the first case (green rectangle) we see a typical hidden bullish divergence, and in the second case (black rectangle) we always see a typical hidden divergence, but this time bearish.

As we can see, the dynamic is identical to the one we described in the paragraph on the RSI, but this time in the green triangle we see that a new low is not marked, and that the peak stops at a price slightly higher than that reached in the previous minimum so that the line joining the two peaks (colored blue) is ascending. We find our beautiful hidden divergence by joining the minimums constructed by the MACD and obtaining a new line (also drawn in blue) which instead moves in the opposite direction (descending). The final outcome, regardless of whether the divergence is hidden or not, is the same: the price starts to rise and goes to retest the maximum peak reached previously.

In the black rectangle, we are instead witnessing a

bearish scenario. Also, this time the second peak fails to overcome the previous one, but stops a little earlier, so much so that the straight line (blue) that we trace by joining the two peaks is descending; on the MACD, we find our hidden divergence, joining the maximum peaks. In fact, our usual blue line this time is ascending.

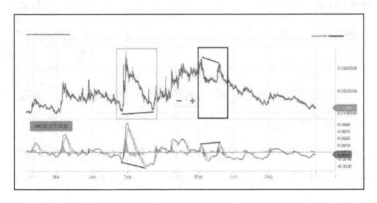

THE ANALYSIS BASIC IN MARKET OF THE CRYPTOCURRENCIES

In the last few chapters, we have introduced some tools commonly considered essential to start trading. We also explained that there are still many other important tools to know how to use, beyond the scope of this text.

We also had the opportunity to explain that a valid trading strategy does not necessarily have to be extremely complicated, but can be extremely simple as long as it is based on rules. A trading strategy is therefore not limited to the tools used for technical analysis, but also includes all those rules that the trader imposes himself with the aim of managing the pressures in the best possible way.

Let's imagine we bought some coins that we don't really know anything about based on simple technical analysisat a price of $10, and we find ourselves 24 hours later with the same coins which dropped to $8. How would we manage the loss? What would happen is that the doubt of having invested in a dying, useless project

176

or on the usual inevitable package would become an exhausting worm that would push us to sell; perhaps in the middle of a dump, perhaps at the lowest possible price (with the greatest possible damage.) It happens more frequently than you might imagine.

If, on the other hand, we had bought some coins that we know well, having analyzed in detail the project on which we invested our money, then enduring a collapse from $10 to $8 becomes easier. However good a trader can be in technical analysis, without fundamental analysis it becomes difficult to trade cryptocurrencies. We have already had the opportunity to explain that in the stock market, fundamental analysis can be understood as the collection of information by reading the company's financial statements, but it is a pity that when we talk about cryptocurrencies most of the time there is no company at all, let alone a budget.

However, there are factors that we can take into consideration, such as market capitalization (market cap.) By capitalization of a cryptocurrency, we simply mean the total amount that we obtain by multiplying the number of coins in circulation by the value of those coins. Another evaluation that we must make in this sense is then to distinguish the maximum supply (21 million coins, for example, if we are talking about BTC) from that available (circulating.) Today, there are about 17,5 million BTC in circulation, compared to a maximum number of coins that will ever end up on the market equal to 21 million.

The quantity of coins in circulation, in relation to the maximum number of coins that the network has budgeted, is one of the factors that we should study for a new cryptocurrency. For a real fundamental analysis, we should be able to disassemble the code of the open source platform and understand how it is made, how it works, and above all if it is well done. There are not many people who have the skills to do a true fundamental analysis of a blockchain project, who know how to "disassemble" the platform and understand how it works. Ordinary people, who do not have great computer skills, therefore have other ways to try to understand if we can trust or not.

The very first things that every cryptocurrency trader wants to know when investing his money are about the community (the nodes and users in the network) and the identity of the people involved in developing the project. When we are faced with a coin that is spent by thousands of people every day and processed by its own blockchain through a sufficiently large and decentralized network of nodes, we are already moderately sure that we are dealing with good starting material.

But there are other details that we are interested in knowing, especially in relation to the team of developers that takes care of carrying out the project. Each cryptocurrency should have its own official website, and within the official website there must necessarily be a section in which the leading figures within the community are mentioned. If there is a company or nonprofit behind a project, then figures such as the CEO, department heads, and other executives should also be indicated.

If, on the other hand, behind a project there is neither a company nor a foundation, then on the website there should be a shred of the "about us" section in which the developers are mentioned. What we need to understand is who are the people most exposed in the project: if they are serious people, if they are established, esteemed or not. In short, the more we know the better.

Obviously, even the project led by a good, brilliant, and capable person can end up shipwrecked, and even "famous" people can throw a package at you. But in general, the quality of any project is always closely linked to the quality of the people who take care of it. If we have a decentralized network worthy of the name, with thousands of users who spend that cryptocurrency every day, a team of developers known and respected internationally, we have a whole series of signals that are very useful for building that indispensible trust that.

However, all this is not enough. It is necessary to know the project in more depth, understand how it works, and what kind of opportunities it is capable of offering. To do this, you start by reading a document ("withe paper") that all the teams disseminate and update periodically, in which all the characteristics and peculiarities of the project should be reported, and it should describe in detail how the technology works.

The withe papers should be understood more as

advertising brochures than as information documents (after all, no one would ever put pen to paper that their project is useless, does not work or has no future.) From reading them we can still obtain useful information; if a certain currency, for example, uses a consensus protocol that I already know and do not trust, then it will make little sense to invest in that cryptocurrency.

If I find that the ambition of this new coin that I want to invest in is simply to be yet another blockchain-based payment system, I will probably think that there are older and more reliable coins to keep an eye on, and that I am not interested in investing the my money on what appears to be only the millionth copy of a true innovation.

If again I discover that the platform on which I want to invest, which on paper offers dozens of very interesting services (from the creation of new tokens to the management of smart contract,) is still far behind the other platforms that preside over the same segment of the market, then I will probably be inclined to want to wait a little longer before investing. On the basis of all this information we collect and the different evaluations that each time directly derive from each different information collected, we develop our conviction about a particular project, we define which coins we trust most and which least, with which we feel comfortable operating and which ones we prefer not to deal with.

Of the eight hundred and more cryptocurrencies available on the market (without counting the tokens), it will be enough to isolate twenty of those we like best and concentrate on looking for our trading signals for only those twenty, Even so, we must understand that fundamental analysis is something that must be carried out on a daily basis, and includes all the information and news gathering activity that we have to do practically every day.

Since news moves the market, arriving first on news means taking an advantage over other traders; to do this, there are a series of very useful operations to do, such as follow the developer accounts on social networks, subscribe to the official newsletters, the telegram channel, participate in discussions on the forums where the community meets. In short, any channel that can provide us with news in advance of other traders must be opened and probed frequently.

Once we have defined a group of cryptocurrencies that we trust, studied their charts, collected information on the technology and the people leading the project, and are ready to intercept any new news and having our own trading strategy made up of precise rules, then we will have all the tools that allow us to trade cryptocurrencies profitably.

6.

MARKET PERSPECTIVES - FUTURE VISIONS

A lthough the recent bearish cycle has, over the last 12 months, burned a large part of the increases received by the entire sector, the prospects for the world of cryptocurrencies in 2021 and for the following years appear to be decidedly rosy. Contrary to what some might argue, there are already numerous use cases for this technology; the benefits for the community are indisputable, and it would be simply crazy to think that all this can return to the magician's cylinder and simply disappear into nothingness.

The banks themselves, on the other hand, are making no secret of wanting to explore the potential offered by the blockchain, as it is becoming increasingly clear that the crypto market is here to stay. Paradoxically, not even a couple of days ago I was reading yet another article in a well-known economic newspaper in which yet another observer on duty compared for the umpteenth time cryptocurrencies to the famous tulip bubble of 1636; all this appears ridiculous, and it is not enough to superimpose a couple of graphs to get out of the embarrassment that making such an absurd statement inevitably entails.

The bubbles, properly called, form in a reasonably short period of time, explode just as quickly, and then never reform again. We can notice such behavior in coins like BTC (or others, among those with the largest market capitalization) only if we accept to isolate what has happened in the last 15 months and ignore everything else.

If the market, on the other hand, were to prove to be capable of reacting as it did in the past, not only the major currencies appear destined to recover the losses accumulated in 2018, but it even seems plausible that they could reach new historical highs. What we really need to ask ourselves when we decide that we might be interested in investing in cryptocurrencies is whether we think that blockchain technology can gain more and more space in the coming years or not. If we stop for a moment to think about what the world will be like in 10, 15, or 20 years, then it becomes difficult to assume that blockchain and DLT technologies can simply disappear from circulation. These innovations already have all the characteristics necessary to make us understand that they are not destined to disappear at all, but that they will finally establish themselves in the long term. If we think of other technologies of the past that have ended up revolutionizing our present, we realize how much time plays a crucial role when we talk about these topics; the inventor of 3D printers, for example, initially struggled to find someone interested in that technology since it seemed to all cost too much and had few practical applications

Today, however, 3D printers have greatly revolutionized the world of industrial production. The same electric cars that have long been branded as a whim for the rich, commonly considered for many years too expensive and difficult to recharge for them to spread on the market, today are pointed to by everyone as the future of transportation.

186

All this seems destined to repeat itself with cryptocurrencies, a technology widely snubbed

by many "experts" on duty who do not seem able to fully understand the revolutionary scope that a technology such as the blockchain carries with it. Therefore, speaking with the detractor of the moment, what we will notice is that our dear friend will inevitably "stick" to the graphs to demonstrate that the price drop is so important that it automatically decrees the death of the market; they will not hear reasons, they will not accept explanations, they will show with absolute certainty all the most disturbing features of the BTCchart, highlighting even the smallest bearish signal to take it right.

What these people have not understood is that normally, those who operate with cryptocurrencies do not care for the price in a moment X. There was a moment, for example, when BTC plunged to $2 after hitting $32. I challenge anyone today not to wish they had bought even a dozen coins for the price of $32; certainly those who bought on that peak had very stressful months later, during which they accumulated painful losses, but those who accepted to play the game in a long-term perspective were able to subsequently take off great satisfaction.

The price, when we talk about cryptocurrencies, is not considered relevant compared to the price we will see in three years. Since what makes the difference with cryptocurrencies is first of all adoption; that is, it all depends on how many people agree to use this technology. The question we should ask ourselves before any other is if in five years the number of people using BTC will be increased or decreased. The answer to this question, based on what we have seen in the last ten years, clearly appears to be that the number of users is destined to increase. Many of the people I know myself could very well start using this technology in the next ten years.

All this does not mean, of course, that there will be no new collapses, with coins that today have an important capitalization and that could instead in a few years completely disappear from the market. But it is baseless to think that the whole market will disappear. If we look at the number of users, what we understand

188

is that the race in recent years, which has made BTC fly up in price, appears to be a small appetizer in consideration of the still small number of people who use this technology

7.

TOOLS AND ADVICE

Being passionate about cryptocurrencies, regardless of whether you decide to also do trading, implies that you have to start to get assiduously informed about the things that happen in this world. If already in any sector, getting informed has already become a demanding activity; in the cryptocurrency sector, collecting news can become exhausting.

Every day new projects are born, new solutions to old problems arise, and news is spread that we must necessarily follow to inform ourselves adequately. Therefore, we must have clear reference points. First of all, we should get into the perspective of ideas that the big (so-called mainstream) newspapers are not the best source to stay informed when it comes to crypto; very often, in fact, those who write in the big newspapers do so "by contract" are invited to write about a topic in vogue in order to satisfy the demand of users without possessing a background to write about that given topic.

This explains the reason why in the major newspapers we often see glaring mistakes. Over time, fortunately, numerous sites and blogs of an informative/popular nature have been created that deal exclusively with cryptocurrencies and feature writers who are experts in the field.

For fairness, I prefer to avoid mentioning these sites; anyone can still easily do an online search and select those four or five sites, commonly considered credible by the whole community, through which to get information. After all, a person who loves football buys a sports newspaper to get information, not one that deals with politics and news. In the same way, if you want to get serious information about cryptocurrencies, you should not read the economic newspapers, but rely on specialized sites who have been dealing with this topic for years now and who make use of the collaboration of people who have studied this technology.

In any case, the main point of reference for the community that works with cryptocurrencies is the Bitcointalk forum, on which you can find all kinds of information and a solution to any type of problem. The community is always very proactive and attentive to helping novice users, provided of course that newbies demonstrate their commitment, actively seeking the information they need, avoiding the famous "ready-to-eat" meal.

For information on coins and tokens on the market, to know the addresses of official websites, information on the supply and on exchanges that allow you to operate with a specific currency, the reference point for the whole community is Coinmarketcap. To get information on technical news, new releases planned, recent technical developments, any expected hard forks and any other purely technical information, it is very common to use a site called Coinmarketcal, much appreciated by traders.

Sites such as Reddit are still very popular with cryptocurrency enthusiasts, and each project normally has its own page on this site. Then there are obviously newsletters and the official communication channels of the various currencies. Social media are also important, so as well as follow the official accounts of the various projects we must also start following the individual developers who often have the opportunity to share real gems through social media; moreover, nowadays it has become very common for traders to share their operations through social networks.The advice, therefore, especially for those who want to trade, is to select a group of trusted traders (based on the quality of the analyzes they are capable of producing) and follow them on the various social networks, trying to understand their trading strategy. By assuming all these small habits, we will slowly begin to orient ourselves by finding figures who represent a point of reference for us, of which we have full confidence, and who will allow us to optimize the little time we have available to be able to inform ourselves.

CONCLUSIONS

We have reached the end of our journey into the world of blockchain technology, and it is time to sum up this path. Obviously, a reading of such a text is not enough to build a deep knowledge of this type of technology, but it should still allow anyone, regardless of their technical skills, to start a path of greater understanding on the basics of trading cryptocurrency.

Knowing briefly how blockchain technology works does not mean knowing the market. You will frequently hear that all the "altcoins" are nothing more than clones of BTC, but this is not the case at all, and to know a specific cryptocurrency you must first study it.

Since the consensus protocols are different, the hash algorithms are different, and the characteristics of the network are different, consequently it is inevitable that every project ends up having unique peculiarities. In order to be able to say that you truly understand the

194

blockchain, therefore, it is inevitable that you have to dedicate some time to an in-depth study of the major cryptocurrencies on the market. In any case, this time will not be wasted, since in the coming years this technology will likely have a heavy impact on our daily lives, redesigning the world as we know it, like the birth of the internet in the 1990s.

Anyone, therefore, who has ever found himself thinking with regret about the birth of the internet, regretting not having been able to immediately seize the opportunities that this new technology was offering, cannot afford the luxury of missing this train again or he will find himself to regret it bitterly in the coming years. That such an opportunity could return in such a short time after the great internet revolution, frankly, it should be understood as something more unique than rare: a coincidence that we have only very rarely seen happen in the course of human history.

It is true that technological development has now become exponential. It is also true that technology moves much faster than we humans can, but currently there is perhaps only one possible area that could prove capable of impacting so strongly on our daily lives, and it is represented by genetics.

What I am arguing, in other words, is that it is not certain that in the next 50 years the possibility of "riding" a new technology that has been so relevant since its inception will reappear. It is already extraordinary that the same generation has had the opportunity to experience two such epochal moments. It is difficult to imagine that in the coming years there will still be a third opportunity in this sense.

The challenge, at this point, consists more than anything else in the form that we will be able to give to this new technological revolution. If we are able to use this type of technology to make the world a better place, or if, even at the expense of technology itself, we will continue to repeat the same mistakes over and over again. In any case, all this strictly depends on us and on the choices we will make (as a people, as citizens) in the coming years.

Accepting, as unfortunately seems to be becoming very common, of losing our right to privacy by sacrificing it to the altar of security and legality, in the long run could prove to be a bad choice capable of generating a series of extremely deleterious effects. With consequences that are difficult to imagine today; what will happen, if we have the courage to use this technology to put people and individuals at the center of the world, instead of limiting ourselves to putting them under permanent control only time will tell us.